BYGONE STORIES
FROM THE
SAN JUAN PROSPECTOR
1885-1886

Karen Ballentine

Dedicated to
Kathy and Fred

INTRODUCTION

November 1886: There is something decidedly fascinating in holding up to the people of other times the lamp of their own civilization and studying them in the light which comes to us, subdued by the flight of time and mellowed by the haze of distance.

Join me for a trip through the "San Juan Country" in 1885 and 1886 via the pages of the *San Juan Prospector*, Del Norte, Colorado. Walk the streets. Climb Lookout Mountain. Meet some of the locals. Discover what day to day life was like in the late 1800s.

The stories include some of everything from the building of an observatory in Del Norte to gunfights in Silverton. Some stories are hilarious and some are tragic, just like they are today, because even though times have drastically changed, these stories will show that people have not. Readers of today can still relate to those folks from the horse and buggy days and maybe even learn a few lessons from them.

The counties that made up the "San Juan Country" are located in southwestern Colorado and include: Ouray, San Juan, Dolores, San Miguel, Hinsdale, Rio Grand, and La Plata. News comes from the cities of Del Norte, Ouray, Silverton, Montrose, Monte Vista, Saguache, Alamosa, and more.

Counties of Southwestern Colorado

Map credit: https://commons.wikimedia.org/wiki/
File:Map_of_Colorado_counties,_labelled.svg

BYGONE STORIES
1885

JANUARY 1885
- January 3, 1885 -

San Juan Siftings

- Ouray and Silverton sleighs make a trip between the two places in four hours. Fare, $5.
- San Juan County is the only county in the State that owns a dance hall and they want to sell it.
- Our city has organized what is known as "The Stuffed Club," an organization devoted to piety and spring chickens.
- Lake City is having trouble with the Eastern mail. Too much snow. D&RG conductors reported it is impossible to get within six miles of Marshall Pass.
- W. W. Durkee of Zapata, a San Luis Valley cattle king, is represented as a desirable catch. He has an old and wealthy uncle with a bad cough and a large bank account. Address: Box 84 Zapata.
- The killing of Tom Cain, at Ash Fork, Arizona, has been confirmed by the Ash Fork postmaster. That settles it. Remarks regarding the gentleman's ancestors and social standing are now in order.

State News

- Pueblo is cursed with burglars and the police don't catch them.
- A letter from Glenwood Springs says that the inhabitants

of that town have not seen in the sun for a month, that it has been raining every day, and that the mud is a foot deep. Such a delightful resort for invalids!

- Miss Nellie Cornish of South Pueblo was seriously burned on Christmas evening while acting as Santa Claus in costume. She was reaching among the lights of a Christmas tree for presents when her clothing caught fire. She was badly burned before the fire was extinguished.

The tramp question has been solved at last. One of those wandering emissaries of evil entered the house of a lady on Long Island and demanded money. She handed him her pocketbook with one hand and shot him dead with a pistol in the other. The verdict of the Coroner's Jury was that he died from exposure.

The new Washington monument is being put to some use. The engineer of the work has made a bet with Hines, the baseball player, that the latter cannot catch a ball tossed from a window 500 feet from the ground. The ball will, it is estimated, make the descent in five and a half seconds and will be moving at the rate of 180 feet per second, or two miles per minute, by the time it reaches Hines' hands. The experiment is looked forward to with much interest.

A debating club at Quincy has decided that it is more fun to see a man thread a needle than a woman drive a nail.

- January 10, 1885 -

San Juan Siftings

- Fun and gradual starvation are reported as the fruits of conducting an aggressive newspaper in Ouray County.
- Del Norte has been boiling over with Saguache people this week.

Probably the most singular curiosity in the book world is a volume that belongs to the family of the Prince de Lague and is now in France. It is entitled "The Passion of Christ," and is neither written nor printed. Every letter of the text is cut out of a leaf and, being interleaved with blue paper, it is as easily read as the best print. The labor and patience bestowed in its completion must have been excessive. The general execution is in every respect is indeed admirable and the volume is of the most delicate and costly kind. Rudolph II of Germany offered 11,000 ducats for it in 1610, which would probably equal $60,000 at this day. The most remarkable circumstance connected with it is that it bears the royal arms of England but when it was in that country and by whom it was owned has never been ascertained.

- January 17, 1885 -

Local News

- Del Norte has a streetcar and street lamp scheme underway.
- There will be a sheet and pillow case masquerade at the rink on the evening of the 23rd. Fun ahead.
- By the way, ladies, Gus Weiss is very fond of pies. He likes a nice big, fat pie better than anything. He is short one pie

this week. Ask him about it.

- Property owners in Del Norte should make arrangements to set out trees, and plenty of them, in the spring. Let us beautify our town. A very small effort on the part of each one will accomplish this end.

San Juan Siftings

- The Durango *Herald* will take ranch produce on accounts. Hard times.
- Durango has a dancing school. Durango newspapers are opposed to fast waltzing.
- Mary, age 18, care of the Montrose *Enquirer*, wishes to correspond with a number of gentlemen. She says she never had a lamb.
- Rico school children are reported so very untidy that the school directors have been obliged to provide soap, towels, combs and brushes in the schools.
- Thousands of copies of *Heart and Hand*, a Chicago matrimonial publication, were wafted into the San Juan country last week to gladden the cabins of many old dyed-in-the-wool bachelors. Ed Howard, at Animas Forks, received a copy and went into spasms.
- Jack Wilson, an eleven years subscriber to the PROSPECTOR renewed his subscription this week.

The average size of an American family is 5.04. We suppose the .04 is the computation of an anticipated increase.

Why may not science yet discover that many other things besides fatal diseases throw out germs and microbes?

I believe that yawning is a microbus pursuit. Haven't you noticed when your Sunday evening girl, about 11:30 p.m., shuts her eyes and opens her mouth until you feel as if you were looking into a churchyard on a dark night, that you are irresistibly compelled to yawn too. She throws out yawn-microbes and you get them in the neck.

This gives me the idea that respectability, cheerfulness, and blues are all the developments of microbes. There are microbes in a handsome suit of clothes. Put them on a shabbily dressed man and he will immediately feel respectable. Let a cheerful man come into your office and talk with you for a few minutes and you become cheerful also. Reasoning from analogy, my theory must be correct and I challenge anyone to prove that it is not.

The highest priced pew in Grace Church, New York, cost the buyer $3000. Salvation comes high back in God's country.

At the sale of pews in Plymouth Church, New York, last week, the cash realized was $27,256. Beecher is pleased.

- January 24, 1885 -

Del Norte has the finest flouring mill in the valley and in this respect is in the lead. While other towns cannot possibly hope to equal Del Norte for years, we should not slack up on our effort to keep years ahead of our sister towns. The San Luis Valley will probably contain one principal town and numerous small ones. Del Norte's enterprise will certainly entitle it to its present position for years to come — the Queen City of the Valley.

With the present number [issue] the PROSPECTOR enters upon the twelfth year of its existence, during almost nine years of which period the present management has been connected with the paper in various capacities. The paper, originally a very modest looking little six-column sheet was started at a time when Del Norte was the center of excitement and the outfitting point for the great San Juan country toward which the eyes of thousands were turned and scores of travelers fairly scampered over the various routes in their haste to become wealthy through the great silver and gold mines of the Southwest. Our old-timers will readily recall the day when the first copy of the PROSPECTOR, the first newspaper published in the State west of the Sangre de Cristo range) was printed in the old log cabin opposite the present site of Young's feed stable; how the boys gathered around to get a glimpse of the wonder, and how the first copy of the paper was auctioned off at a good price to the highest bidder. Those were exciting days. During these eleven years the PROSPECTOR has seen the country pass through the boom, joys and sorrows of all Western sections. It has seen the old-timers become wealthy or poor, seen them live or die, locate with us or remove to a new country, and the PROSPECTOR, like a faithful pilot at the helm, advocating the settlement and what it believed to be for the good of the county. In return it has enjoyed the good will of the people at large both at home and abroad. The PROSPECTOR has become a newspaper firmly planted in a section which it will ever strive to faithfully represent. The mines, the agricultural and pastoral possibilities are in better shape today than they ever were and with the addition of excellent educational and mercantile facilities, the addition of hundreds of new settlers, with the busy hum of industry on all sides, who cannot see the almost total fulfillment of the prophecies and hopes of those hardy pioneers who laid out our town and did the first hard work toward the establishment of what is now the Queen City of the San Luis Valley. In entering our twelfth year, the PROSPECTOR is fully as confident of the ultimate outcome of the little city of Del Norte and the San Luis Valley as were the prospectors who camped upon and laid out our town site years ago.

From pretty much everybody who have paid taxes lately come complaints of the size of the assessment. The rate is high — there can be no question about that. There is, of course, only one course open to us now and that is the old-fashioned forgotten way of bringing our expenses within our income. The County commissioners must see to it that the county expenses are cut down to the lowest figures on which the county can be run. The claim for every dollar must be rigorously scrutinized and if improper, promptly disallowed. Economy must now be the order of the day until our public affairs are brought back into respectable shape. There are no two ways as to what must be done.

A short time ago 21 young men in a northern county in Missouri were out on a lam and during the fun it was proposed that all should get married on a certain day in the future. This was agreed to. One of the party offered to wager that in ten years from the marriage he would have more children than any one of the other 20. Another and finally all entered into the same kind of a bet, swelling the purse to $1,050 to go to the person having the largest family in ten years. Strange as it may seem, the 21 young men have so far succeeded. Christmas was set as the day of the marriage and a grand banquet was given. And still the State goes Democratic.

A recent application to the President-elect was addressed to "His Majesty, Grover Cleveland." The writer wants an Illinois post office [job].

Local News

- Justice Young has everything in shape to deal out the law to evil-doers. Office at his grain rooms, Columbia Avenue. Matrimonial knots a specialty.
- A new rink-le in the roller-skating mania in adjoining towns is a race between boys who crawl through barrels and eat pies while making the race. In another race the contestants jump hurdles and pull off their boots upon the course.
- From Dr. Norman Chapman, who has lately arrived from Summitville, we learn that there is every reason for supposing that the Annie mill will continue running through the winter. Everything is working nicely. Sleighs run daily to Baker's place and wagons from that point to Del Norte.

San Juan Siftings

- "Deep snows, nothing doing, and no money" is the wail from Silverton.
- Alamosa was full of cattle men last week — witnesses in the Carter case.
- Alamosa wants a starch factory — a rather stiff suggestion considering the condition of the money market.
- The first engine ever built in the San Juan country was turned out by the Durango iron works recently.

- Harry Wright lately rode a snow-slide several hundred feet in Hinsdale County. He was dug out by Bill Richards.
- Thus far this winter, San Juan snow slides have not succeeded in killing the usual number of men. Let us hope that it remains so.
- Some wicked San Juan exchanges have lately stolen original poetry from the *Register* of Lake City, without credit. A man who is mean enough to steal skating rink poetry will do almost anything.
- Thirteen snowshoers "hooked up" to a sleigh, pulled Mrs. Ed Brown from Mineral Point to Ouray recently, over the mountains. The lady was ill with rheumatism. Her child was strapped upon the father's back during the same journey.
- The Durango *Idea* objects to fast waltzing. We would just like to swing around the room once or twice with the *Idea*. That's our style — a slow four-o-clock in the morning waltz every time.
- Pete Barclay threatened to burn a $1,000 bill if Teller was elected. Terrible waste of cash. Send it around to the country newspapers.

- January 31, 1885 -

We are sorry to note the actions of a number of boys and young men in Del Norte, who persist in the use of obscene language and commit all manner of depredations in the business and residence portions of our town. These young men and boys, almost without exception, are of good parentage and there can be no possible excuse for their actions. They annoy our businessmen and social gatherings by their rude actions and speech. The names of many of these offenders have been handed in to the town authorities who may take action in the matter at an early day.

Jim Williams and Dr. Rapp made their debut on roller skates at the rink last Tuesday evening. Mr. Williams did not exhibit the poetry of motion to any great extent while Dr. Rapp was a howling triumph.

San Juan Siftings

- Durango is inaugurating a movement for the benefit of the poor.
- Silverton has a double scandal. It is about time for a killing in that camp.
- Heads of happy homes in Denver have taken down the old shotguns during the presence of various Silvertonians in the city.
- Telluride will have a tri-weekly mail and four-horse coaches after May 1. Telluride will be a live camp.
- Snow on Poncha Pass lately left Saguache without mail for a week.
- Mayor D. R. Smith, of Alamosa, has been arraigned by the balance of the Board of Trustees charged with various misdemeanors not entirely in keeping with the dignity of his position. Mr. Smith signified his willingness to answer all charges.

One of the cleverest hoaxes ever perpetrated was invented by Dean Swift and intended for the public good. He caused to be printed and circulate some "last works" of a street robber named Elliston, purporting to be written shortly before his execution in which the condemned thief was made to say —

"Now, as I am a dying man, I have done something which may be of good use to the public. I have left with an honest man — the only honest man I was ever acquainted with — the names of all my wicked brethren, the places of their abode, with a short account of the crimes they have committed, in many of which I have been their accomplice and heard the rest from their own mouths. I have likewise set down the names of those whom we call our setters, of the wicked houses we frequent and all of those who receive and buy our stolen goods. I have solemnly charged this honest man, and have received his promise upon oath, that whenever he hears of any rogue to be tried for robbery or housebreaking he will look into his list. If he finds the name there of the thief concerned, he is to send the whole paper to the Government. Of this I here give my companions fair and public warning and hope they will take it."

The Dean's ruse succeeded so well that street robberies were for many years after few and far between.

FEBRUARY 1885
- February 7, 1885 -

Local News

- Long live the Queen City with her college, courteous residents, fine public schools, churches, saw and planing mill, sash factory, mercantile houses, etc.
- Our County Commissioners have applied for permission to plank the railroad bridge over the Rio Grande above South Fork for the accommodation of wagon travel.
- One more week and St. Valentine's worshippers will be in the height of their glory. The usual number of ludicrous and elegant valentines are upon exhibition in our show windows.
- The new instruments — two clarinets and a piccolo — for the Del Norte band, have arrived together with a lot of orchestra music. We would be pleased to see our musicians now organize a string band.
- The roof and cupola upon Rio Grande County's courthouse are finished and the building presents a very neat and substantial appearance.

San Juan Siftings

- Charlie Peek has undertaken the task of kissing all the babies in Lake City. He is a candidate for Mayor.
- The office of Alamosa's Mayor has been declared vacant owing to certain alleged misconduct on the part of that

individual. He is charged with several misdemeanors.

- In a Lake City case last week, wherein a certain party and his wife were arraigned for selling liquor without a license, the wife was finally convicted after a series of trials and the certain party discharged. In endeavoring to hold the wife, against the warnings of the counsel for the defense and in accordance with the decision of the court, the Marshal was attacked by the husband, who swept the ground with the law's representative and took the wife home. At last accounts, the court and city fathers were in one of the county vaults, armed to the teeth, holding a council of war. The majesty of the law received a black eye.

- The Western Mill and Express Company's sleighs or coaches have entered Summitville via the Del Norte route nine-tenths of the days of the present winter. Pineapples do not grow along this route but the traveler over the Western Mail and Express Company's line get there every time.

- February 14, 1885 -

San Juan Siftings

- E. Easterly has been elected to the position of Mayor of Alamosa in place of D. R. Smith, removed.

- Alamosan's are discussing the question of straightening the course of the Rio Grande River at that point with a view to protecting the town against it.

War on roller skating rinks is being waged by clergymen in several of the towns of northern Ohio.

A school mistress in Barry County, Michigan, was dismissed because she declined to eat fat pork, the people believing that she was attempting to put on "too much style."

- February 21, 1885 -

Local News

- The train from the East arrived six hours late last Tuesday. Cause, burning of a bridge between Denver and Pueblo.
- There was no mail from Lake City from Friday of last week to Tuesday of this, caused by a carrier throwing up the contract.

San Juan Siftings

- The Durango and Silverton papers, in the absence of all other news, give up most of their space to reports of the skating rink exercises.
- The Telluride brass band visited Rico last week on snowshoes and regaled the citizens of the latter place with some excellent music.
- Rico has had but five deaths in the last five years. Of these, two were murdered, two lynched, and one fell down a shaft. Healthy place.
- The Rico *News* says Jim Sullivan, who killed Ike Stockton in Durango while the latter was resisting arrest, was seen by some of his Colorado acquaintances at the New Orleans Exposition the other day. He has quit all his wild and wooly ways, is very quiet, and is physically a complete wreck of his former self. The fact that the Jim Sullivan alluded to above died near Chama over a year ago causes us to doubt the accuracy of this story. — *Durango Herald*

14

It is well to say right here that the bill to regulate Pullman fares should be defeated. The Legislature has no power to meddle with through rates and the tariff within the State, at least on the Denver & Rio Grande, is low enough.

"This thing's got to stop!" said Archie Williams, the U. P. Attorney. "This newspaper (holding up a Denver daily) came out and refers to me as Archer Williams, the most villainous of names, and to cap the climax of infamy, it says I am from Omaha! I've got to draw the line somewhere and d_____d if I don't draw it a little this side of Omaha."

The PROSPECTOR is pleased to note the improved typography and general excellence of the Alamosa *Journal* and is led to imagine that its patronage is large and increasing. The *Journal* deserves all that it gets and a great deal more. At a time when the whole of Conejos County was under the control of a corrupt clique of politicians and honesty was at a premium, the *Journal* initiated a contest against them which is now good and won. The *Journal* had made for itself a record of which it may well be proud and for which the taxpayers of Conejos County may well be grateful.

The Silver convention brought to the surface more cranks than it was thought the State held. Some of them are still keeping up a desultory fire in the newspapers. One of them writes to the Georgetown *Courier* that the convention was "packed" by Governor Grant and others in the interest of Wall Street. It is a pity that the insane asylum at Pueblo cannot be packed in the interest of people who are tired of hearing such nonsense.

A Letter From Aspen from a Former Citizen of Del Norte

I suppose that your readers will be somewhat disappointed when they read this letter, but I have been very careful to find out the facts in every instance and what statements I may make are based upon those facts and information that I have every reason to believe reliable.

Aspen is located at the junction of the Roaring Forks of the Grand River and Castle Creek, in Pitkin County, Colorado, at a distance of forty-five miles from the town of Granite on the D&RG railway, and about forty miles from Glenwood Springs.

There is really more of a boom about Aspen in other parts of the State than there is at Aspen itself, and there is really more of a boom here than the facts seem to warrant. It is true that there are a number of good paying mines here and the output of these alone is in the neighborhood of $2,500 a day.

There are probably 4,000 people in the town now and they keep coming in very rapidly. About nine-tenths of them are in a distressed financial condition when they get here and very few of them make an effort to get employment although there seems to be work enough for those that want it. Miners get $3.50 and $4 per day. Mechanics of all kinds are in good demand and get good pay but this state of affairs cannot last long.

As is always the case, town property has doubled and redoubled in value several times in the last three or four months. Any kind of a lot in the business portion of town is worth from $1,000 to $4,000 or more.

There are no less than fifty saloons in operation and a number of them never close their doors. Wheels of Fortune, Roulette, Keno, Faro, and every table game known to the knights of the green cloth, make and break (mostly break) men nightly.

The traffic between here and Granite is considerable, freight teams going out loaded with ore and bullion and coming in with supplies. There are on the road about eighty 4s and fifteen to twenty 6s, mostly mule teams and all freighting is done with sleds.

The day I came over from Granite, the coaches started with eighteen passengers and at Twin Lakes were met by the Leadville coach with fourteen more. We passed about sixty more on the road. What is to become of most of them, I have not the least idea.

They have a very good skating rink and opera house combined and another one is being built.

In conclusion, I will say that in my opinion this is one of the few mountain towns that a railroad will benefit and would make a number of what are now valueless properties valuable. — Ed A. Clemons

Paul Hines, Snyder, Baker and Yewell are persevering and have made several attempts to catch a baseball thrown from the Washington monument. In one instance a ball was thrown off for Snyder to catch but he was unable to judge it correctly. Hines, who happened to be several yards distant, saw the ball coming his way, put up his gloved hands, but the sphere went through them like a flash and made a deep indentation in the frozen ground. Phil Baker captured the ball once unexpectedly but only held it momentarily. There seems to be no rule by which the ball falling from such a great distance can be judged. — *Chicago Inter Ocean*

Congressmen are each paid salaries of $5000 a year. There are 325 of them and about 25 of that number are worth their salaries.

The newspapers are having a terrible time trying to get the name of a Colorado town right. The town is Saguache and it has been brought into notice by a railway accident in which a citizen of Saguache was killed. The local papers got the town as San Sache, San Gache, San Gauche, Saint Goche, and San Chole. By the way, the Colorado people pronounce the name of Saguache as if it were spelled Siwatch. — *Chicago News*

Henry [Monte Vista]. St. Valentine's Day was very breezy, being the most disagreeable day we have had for nearly a year past. Very little attention was given to the observance of the day as a holiday.

A bill is pending in the Rhode Island Legislature providing for the creation of a new holiday to be known as Veteran's Day, the idea being a day for a general reunion of veteran Union soldiers.

- February 28, 1885 -

The "Adamless Eden" troupe closed a week's engagement at the Tabor Grand last week and Denver's high moral principles have again resumed their normal condition.

Diseases of the type of scarlet fever which have visited Del Norte during the last year may be attributed directly to the neglect of sanitary precautions in the matter of the proximity of wells and cesspools. If there is a town ordinance governing the subject, it should be enforced. If there is not, one should be passed. The pure air of this elevation will not preserve health when the drinking water is poisoned.

- Rico is to have a brass band.
- Montrose claims a population of 1200.
- Ouray consumed $118,000 worth of whiskey and $480 worth of religion last year.
- This has been the mildest winter seen in the San Juan country for years.
- Silverton has pulled through another week without a scandal.

The dedication of the Washington Monument took place on the 21st.

MARCH 1885
- March 7, 1885 -

The PROSPECTOR has stood the test for eleven years and still stands as a representative of the people. Was not the Henry *Graphic* established in the interests of a corporation that seeks to control our heretofore peaceful valley? Is it not plain that the *Graphic* wishes to gain control of the reins of government with a view to turning them over to its master — the corporation? In view of this fact, it behooves our people to be on the alert. We want a government established by the people and not by a corporation.

The *Graphic* is tooth and nail against Del Norte and the general welfare of Rio Grande County.

The "Sunny San Luis Valley" will receive a large percent of the State's new settlers during the coming summer.

San Juan Siftings
- Progressive euchre has invaded Alamosa.
- The total snowfall thus far in Lake City is 58 inches.
- Frank Hyatt, Alamosa's popular Marshal, is one of the best men in his line in the Southwest.
- Durango Methodists accepted a benefit at the rink last week. Skating in a Martha Washington costume will not be sanctioned by some of our church-going people.

The difference in the nervous condition of authors is quite as great as the difference in their methods of working. One writer cannot endure the presence of either wife or child, while another is totally unmoved by the frolics of his family. Tom Hood wrote generally at night when all was quiet and the children were asleep. "I have a room to myself," he exclaimed in a letter describing a change of lodgings, "which will be worth 20 pound to me, for a little noise disconcerts my nerves." Even a separate room, however, will not always secure absolute quiet. "I remember," writes one, "being in company pervaded by the breezy presence of Anthony Trollope. Someone was talking of the Franco-German War and of its practical issues." "There is one thing it did," Trollope said, striking in with his loud voice and hearty manner, "It took away all the German bands from London and many of them never came back."

As with most people who work with pen or pencil, a German band was death to a day's work with Trollope. Oddly enough, it was to one of these curses of civilization that his death was more or less owing. A little more than a month before he died, a German band arranged itself outside his house and struck up its soul destroying noise. Trollope sent a servant to order it off. The men would not go and Trollope, leaving his work, went out and had a row with the leader of the band. Thus the delicate state of his health and the same night, at the dinner table of his brother-in-law, he had the seizure which ended fatally.

- March 14, 1885 -

Rev. Darley dismissed his congregation last Sunday evening owing to the fire alarm. The congregation was the largest for many weeks. When a man is in church and hears the fire alarm, it is safer to pass out via the aisles than to endeavor to jump over the pews, and more refined.

Arrangements are now underway by the Trustees of the Presbyterian College of the Southwest at Del Norte, looking toward the construction of an observatory upon the top of Mount Lookout, 700 feet above the town. It is expected to have the work completed by September next.

Later: A force of men began work on the excavation for the observatory building Friday morning. It is expected that a large force of men will begin work on the road up the mountain Monday morning. All parties feeling like aiding this project can best do so by reporting upon the grounds with a pick and shovel next Monday morning at 7 o'clock.

San Juan Siftings

- No scandals reported from Silverton this week.
- Eleven houses have been erected under the San Luis Valley Canal within a few weeks.
- Ouray newspapers are again at war. Rio Grande is the only county in the State where white-winged peace angel flaps her wings over the press gang.

- March 21, 1885 -

The *Graphic* says that the saloons in Del Norte have been reduced in number to five, and that there is a growing sentiment here in favor of "soberiety" — whatever that may be.

The PROSPECTOR has been guilty of the damnable offense of defending the good name and property of the people of its town and county against the assaults of a corporation organ. For this, the people not under the leash of the Loan and Trust company are branded as a "ring" and the PROSPECTOR as their "organ."

- March 28, 1885 -

A large number of our citizens who have subscribed to Rev. Darley's salary will do well to waltz around and pay up. A minister cannot live on scenery. Give the parson a lift — he deserves it.

R. C. Nisbet lately shipped potatoes from Del Norte at eight cents per hundred weight by the car load.

Soap, marbles and chalk are legal tender at Rico.

The Henry Mountain fraud is being exposed every day. It is a safe section to stay away from.

The Alamosa Mayorality trouble had its final hearing this week but we have not yet learned its final disposal.

St. Patrick's Day was celebrated at Rico in style. A notable feature of the procession was the scarcity of Irishmen.

For some time past, a number of boys from fifteen to eighteen years of age have been committing various depredations in and around Del Norte, their operations culminating last Monday in the arrest of Henry and August Born, Charlie Lum, John Tefft, and

Edson Horner.

These boys, excepting Horner, were arraigned before Justice of the Peace Chas. Young last Tuesday afternoon and bound over to the District Court in the sums following their names for the following causes.

August Born, for being one of a party who recently set fire to Burton's blacksmith shop, $1,000 bond.

Henry Born, for setting fire to Burton's blacksmith shop and stealing sacks from Middaugh's store to the value of $20, $1,000 bond.

John Tefft, for stealing sacks from Middaugh's store to the value of $20, $500 bond.

Charlie Lum, for robbing the contribution box at the Presbyterian Church, $300 bond.

Edson Horner, owing to illness, was not brought into court but as he was a party to robbing the contribution box at the Presbyterian Church, his bond will probably be fixed the same as Lum's, $300.

In default of bail, these boys (Horner, Aug. Born, and Lum excepted) were committed to jail to await the action of the Grand Jury which has been called for Friday, the 27th inst.

Comment upon these cases is unnecessary — they speak for themselves. While we regret exceedingly that such things should happen within the limits of our town, the action of the authorities in the premises is just and proper. The Penitentiary or Reform School will most likely be the lot of the entire crowd. The cases are clear and if the law is enforced, there can be but one end to this chapter of crime.

Robert Chase, who was present when the building above

referred to was fired, gave the information which led to the arrest of the firebugs, who gave evidence entangling the church robbers and sack thieves. To Marshal James Murray, perhaps more than any other, belongs the credit of having worked up these cases.

Later

Upon complaint of Carl Born, father of the boys above named, a warrant was issued for Robt. Chase Tuesday evening upon the charge of having set fire to the Burton building, and was served by Deputy Sheriff Sawyer. A trial was demanded at once by young Chase's friend, which Justice Young declined to grant and Chase was set at liberty upon the personal guarantee of citizens that he would be ready for trial at 10 a.m. on Wednesday, the 25th inst. Attorney Maguire refused to prosecute this case and tendered his services in its defense. The defendant appeared with his attorney and sureties before Justice Young on Wednesday morning and gave bail in the sum of $500.

News from Summitville — I wish I could write you a newsy letter for a change, but just now everyone is so very quiet in this burgh that something new and interesting is at a premium.

Blasting will be continued every day in various places along the new road to the summit of Mt. Lookout and parents may avoid accidents by keeping their children away from the hill.

The latest authority on the vexed question of sleep, Dr. Malins, says that the proper amount of sleep to be taken by a man is eight hours. So far as regards city life the estimate is probably correct. Proverbial wisdom does not apply to modern conditions of social existence.

"Five for a man, seven for a woman, and nine for a pig" says one proverb.

"Nature requires five, custom gives seven, laziness takes nine and wickedness eleven" says Mr. Hazlitt in his English Proverbs.

These conclusions were, however, drawn from observation of country life. Physical fatigue is more easily overcome than intellectual. Men, however, who follow any intellectual pursuit are exceptionally fortunate if the processes of restoration occupy less than seven hours; more frequently it extends to eight or nine hours.

More than 100 persons, it is reported, have been indicted at St. Mary's, West Virginia, for playing dominoes in public.

APRIL 1885
- April 4, 1885 -

The Colorado legislature is made up as follows:

- In the Senate there are six miners, six stock growers, five merchants, one banker and eight lawyers.
- In the House there are six miners, nine stock growers, three ranchmen, fifteen lawyers, six merchants, two hotel men and one of each of the following: Banker, surveyor, editor, real estate dealer, brewer and machinist.

The sermon at the Presbyterian Church next Sabbath evening will be to boys and young men and is taken from Proverbs 27:11 — "My son, be wise." In the face of recent developments in the city, we trust the house will be crowded. No more suitable text could be chosen at the present time.

San Juan Siftings

- A lot of boys at Saguache were fined $5 each for being too funny last week.
- Harry Leroy returned from the Henry Mountain (Utah) boom last week and reports it a large body of sandstone carrying copper stain and woodchuck holes.

The Grand Jury

- In the cases of Henry Born, Aug. Born, and Robt. Chase, arson, true bills were found as to the first two named.

- In the case of Charlie Lunn, upon charge of robbing the contribution box at the Presbyterian Church, no bill was found, owing probably to the boy's youth.
- In the case of H. Born and Jno. Tefft, grand larceny, true bills were found.
- In the case of Robert Born, Harry Jones and others, charged with an assault upon a female in West Del Norte, true bills were found as to Born and Jones.
- Edson Horner, who was implicated in the Presbyterian robbery and the sack stealing, has skipped but will probably be found.
- The Grand Jury visited the jail, recommended that it be cleaned out, celled, better ventilation secured and that a ten-foot high board fence be built around the jail building.

District Court Sentences

Henry Born, for arson, was sentenced to the Reform School for four years. Jno. Tefft, grand larceny, to the Industrial school for three years.

- April 11, 1885 -

The Queen City of the Valley sends greetings to her sister cities and extends to them an invitation to gaze upon the beauties of nature from her observatory — when it is completed.

Work on the road to the summit of Mt. Lookout will be nearly completed this week. The wagon road proper will be twelve feet wide and 2,100 feet long. The steepest grade will be fifteen feet in one hundred while the average grade is probably from two to ten feet in one hundred.

On the summit, rock has been blasted out for a reception room 14x20 and an observatory building 20x20. The buildings are being framed and will be erected just as soon as the road is completed. The museum building will be built on the point at the end of the wagon road.

The view from the top of Lookout is grand in the extreme. The Sangre de Cristo range looms up for a distance of one hundred miles, while the Rio Grande River can be traced to New Mexico with the naked eye. Away off to the northward and eastward lie the canals of the Colorado Loan and Trust company. The town of Henry, fifteen miles away, can be distinctly seen, while with an ordinary glass, Alamosa, thirty miles away, and old Fort Garland, sixty-five miles away, and the Spanish Peaks, one hundred miles away, may be seen. In the background is one of the grandest mountain ranges upon the continent, its needles looming skyward and almost piercing the heavens, while in the valley below, amid the streaks of sunlight and shadow, hundreds of new homes are going up.

To say that this work will be beneficial to our town is drawing it mildly. This observatory will draw sightseers from all over the world when it is known that the Lookout station will be the highest observatory in the world. The observatory will be provided with one of the finest telescopes in the land and a light, probably electric, will be placed upon the summit of the hill.

Too much praise cannot be bestowed upon Mr. Darley, who has been principal in this work. It is enterprise of this nature that has made Del Norte what it now is and it should be encouraged.

Sheriff Jordan and posse returned from Canon City and Golden Wednesday, whither they went to deliver Arnold Howard, John Tefft, and Henry Born to the authorities — the former to the State Penitentiary and the two latter to the Industrial School. Howard was placed in the stone quarry. The boys were dressed in regulation costume and will probably be placed at some light work at the Industrial School.

Work on the Court House is progressing nicely. The basement is partially plastered, the first story is all plastered, and by the time the PROSPECTOR is issued, the second story will probably be plastered also. The new vault doors are fine ones. The Clerk and Recorder's office will probably be completed first. Now let some enterprising Del Norte citizen donate a bell for the Court House.

Rev. Darley's sermon, "My son, be wise," last Sunday evening, drew a large congregation.

Alamosa people are holding Del Norte up as a model of all that is perfect. Thank you, gentlemen. We will try to merit it.

A pair of twins were recently born in Del Norte, weighing respectively ten and nine pounds, to Mr. and Mrs. Flannigan, and in these hard times, too.

The large lamp has been placed in position in front of the Presbyterian Church, and is a great improvement upon total darkness, heretofore enjoyed.

- Ouray has three churches, but not one preacher.
- Telluride people who have returned from the Henry Mountains are disgusted.

A curious burial custom is practiced by an old Virginia family, the Fendals of Alexandria. Whenever a member of the family dies, the male representative of the older branch thereof, just before the hour of interment, buries a dagger in the heart of the dead to assure himself of no reawakening. The dagger used is one sacred to the purpose and has been devoted to its use for many generations. The custom originated because of the burial alive of a member of the family and an inherited tendency to a peculiar form of heart disease.

Three hundred pairs of roller skates, it is stated, are now manufactured in this country each month.

Good Friday is a legal holiday in all but four States — Louisiana, Minnesota, Florida and Pennsylvania.

There are fifty-two more patients in the Nevada Hospital for the Insane than there are inmates in the State Prison.

The mail carrier between Lenoir, Tennessee and Stratford, North Carolina, now in his eighty-second year, is said to have carried the mail on that route every day for the last seventy years.

- April 18, 1885 -

The County Commissioners will probably have the stairway continue from the courtroom floor of the Court House to the cupola. Ladies, this is for your benefit — the gentlemen can climb a ladder.

San Juan Siftings

- Durango has an amateur brass band — another point in favor of the Montrose route.
- Col. F.M. Snowden, of Silverton, cleaned out his cabin last week — the first time in four years.
- Saguache County sportsmen have been warned not to shoot any more cats in the town limits.
- J. Christ has accepted a position as superintendent of Durango's public schools. The name sounds familiar.
- Two scandals at Silverton last week were suppressed, owing to the "respectability" of the parties concerned.
- The latest news from Ouray is to the effect that Dave Day is in imminent danger of being scalped for taking a stand against vice.
- The grief parties who do the pang-of-woe business upon the Durango press are glittering triumphs in their line. Durango offers better obituaries than any town in the state. [Editor's note: I could not find a Durango newspaper for this time period.]
- The Alamosa *Journal* says: "Hands have been joined over the bloody chasm," intimating, we infer, that the differences between that paper and certain citizens have been settled.

- A stranger arrived at the Dixon House, Ouray, last week, and during the noon meal took occasion to eat pie with a knife — that is, actually put the end of a case knife blade in his mouth. Three other men at the table fainted, the waiter girl had a spasm, and the porter threw up his job, owing to the class of people he was obliged to come in contact with. Eating pie with a knife is only excelled as a crime in Ouray County by voting the pin-tail ticket.

- April 25, 1885 -

Del Norte has about one foot of snow this Friday morning. Snow has been falling to a greater or lesser extent all week.

Del Norte is working for electric lights.

Remember this is Arbor Day. Plant trees.

The observatory building was constructed in sixteen sections and carried up from the end of the wagon road to the summit of Lookout. The first wagon load was taken up last Monday.

A man came to our office the other day and hinted at a scandal in the city but left us in darkness. We do not believe there is any scandal in our fair city.

If some of the married ladies of the town will look through their husbands' pocketbooks, they will find pictures that have no business there. A large lot came through the mails Monday.

- Alamosa is starting a dancing school.
- Hell hath no fury like a town election — in Ouray.
- Silverton had a cow-hiding scrape last week, says the *Miner*. Racy developments are hinted at.
- The bottom is out of the roads leading into Lake City. Mail carriers on the Del Norte route have been obliged to go a-foot for eight miles along Willow Creek east of Powderhorn.
- Ninety candidates for the Silverton Marshalship met at an out-of-the-way place to take a vote and see who should receive the support of all. Each man voted for himself and the meeting adjourned.

Newsletters, in manuscript, were sold before newspapers were printed. The Italian name *Gazette* was first applied to those letters and afterward to the printed copies.

Husbands and wives only learn by experience how much happiness they add to their daily lives by thinking twice before speaking once. This particularly when they have a hateful or simple sentence behind their teeth. When respect and confidence are thoroughly established, many a little suggestion and bit of advice from one or the other is received in a most charming way. He is an anomalous young husband who does not need topping off here and there. Only a little twig, maybe, but enough to mar the domestic oak if the pruning knife is not used. It is so natural to hold a wife responsible for her husband's toilette and social failings that these two things alone cause an immense amount of domestic warfare unless the opposing forces are under a loving flag of truce. A wife, too, can annoy her husband so much that it takes the opera, the club, or a wrestling match to make him forget the ties that bind him. A happy family is really a training school. If the members do not all insist on being professors at the same time, the discipline tells its new story in happy faces, good breeding and hospitality.

MAY 1885
- May 2, 1885 -

Del Norte is among the most pleasant villages in Colorado in which to rear a brood of kids. Good schools, churches, and society. — Ouray *Muldoon*. Henry *Graphic*, please copy.

The PROSPECTOR seems to be tickling nearly everybody in this part of the country with the hope of office, a new method of obtaining subscribers. — Henry *Graphic*

William Bingel, the brewer, has planted over 500 trees upon his place this spring. Of the trees planted, 150 are cherry, plum and apple trees. This is an example worthy of emulation.

- May 9, 1885 -

If you've anything to grieve you,
And fill your heart with fears,
If poverty bides near you,
And your days are dimmed with tears,
If you find, with soul despairing,
No answers to your prayers,
Don't say a word about it
For Nobody really cares!

San Juan Siftings

- A cow thief held up a Durango official last week with a piñon pistol and escaped.
- Rumor says there is a movement afoot to remove the county seat of Conejos County from Conejos to La Jara.
- The Alamosa *Journal* is firing conundrums at its readers and offers a subscription to the paper as a reward for solving them.
- A number of Silverton men joined the Good Templar's Lodge last week and the next day took a drink together in celebrating the event. They were promptly ousted by the lodge, as they should have been.
- Silverton had a Mother Hubbard (get the gun) promenade at the rink last week and the ladies showed their good sense by not appearing in M. H. costume. The prize for the neatest costume (a pair of bracelets) was shelved.

Men are at work getting out rock for the foundation of the Presbyterian College at Del Norte.

Mt. Lookout was thronged with visitors last Sunday. Horses were ridden to the summit and foot passengers swarmed along the road. The observatory is bound to draw.

- May 16, 1885 -

Parties are respectfully asked to refrain from writing names upon the observatory building on Lookout. A register will be provided in due time for names. Wait awhile.

- The Henry *Graphic* is showing signs of a very precarious existence.
- A long range fight is going on between Durango and Ouray newspapers.
- San Juaners who are looking forward to Aspen will do well to bear in mind that smallpox has broken out in the town.
- Ouray's Mayor smokes a corncob pipe, wears his hat on the back of his head, spells council with a "k," and in points of wisdom discounts an owl looking down a rat hole for grub. — *Muldoon*

- May 23, 1885 -

Del Norte has cleaned up her streets and alleys this spring in fine shape. A large number of new dwelling houses and miles of new ditches have been built. An observatory on top of Mount Lookout and a wagon road from the base to the summit has been built. 1,500,000 feet of logs are thundering down the Rio Grande for the Del Norte saw and planing mills. 500,000 bricks will be burned. Two thousand trees have been set out in the town and upon its borders. Good wagon roads from Del Norte to all parts of the country are already built. Long live the Queen City!

The census enumerators will begin their work June 1.

Arrangements are now complete for the proper observance of Memorial Day at Del Norte. It is to be hoped all will observe this day in the proper manner.

San Juan Siftings

- Saguache is full of checker players whose highest ambition is to "skunk" everything in town.
- "I must have order in this courtroom," sternly demanded a Silverton justice of the peace. "I must and will have less noise and confusion here. I have already disposed of three important cases without being able to hear one word of the evidence."
- We are pleased to note a disposition among many parents in Del Norte to place their boys at some useful employment at times while many other boys are idle. Every boy, if possible, should learn a trade and fit himself for usefulness in life. Too many Western boys grow up in ignorance of the responsibilities of life after leaving the home roof.

- May 30, 1885 -

From information given us, we are led to suspect that a certain gentleman in this county is secretly conducting, under the smoke of the general engagement, a fight against the PROSPECTOR. We have no wish to attack a private citizen and do not want to be provoked to such a course. Therefore, we give notice that we will tolerate no bushwhacking. This may not be a word to the wise, but it had better be sufficient.

The Del Norte observatory can be distinctly seen from Alamosa, thirty miles away, with the naked eye.

A man was badly injured near Henry last week by a blow from a pumpkin. He had just planted a pumpkin seed and before he could retire, a full blown pumpkin shot up out of the ground and struck him in the stomach. His cries brought aid just in time to prevent the vines from strangling him to death. Horrible affair, but we must look for anything at this altitude and with this soil.

The courtroom in the new Court House has been painted a very dingy brown color.

San Juan Siftings

- Bicycles are said to be crippling the horse market at Saguache.
- Saguache observed Decoration Day this year for the first time in the history of the town.
- A little son of Mr. and Mrs. R. J. Carson of Durango was stolen from their home last week and no trace has been found. Suspicion now points to an Italian beggar woman, who has been arrested.

JUNE 1885
- June 6, 1885 -

"Revive us again!" The Denver Methodists have rented the rink for the month of July for the purpose of holding a revival under the management of the boy preacher, Harrison. There is ever the prospect of the affair being successful and surely no more needy place than Denver could be found in the State for holding a revival.

San Juan Siftings

- Antelope are reported grazing in the streets of Gunnison.
- A history of San Juan is being written by Gid Propper, of the Telluride *News*.
- A Saguache attorney has left the town, his wife and some debts. So says the *Chronicle*.
- The editor of the Silverton *Miner* recently attended a Spiritual seance and was converted to the faith.
- Since Dave Day "struck it" in Dexter No. 2, every newspaper man in San Juan has concluded to invest his surplus in mines.
- Silverton newspapers complain of the tendency of citizens to carry concealed weapons and ask the authorities to stop the practice.
- Some of the San Juan newspapers are at war with the toll roads of the country. The papers claim that toll roads are doing much to retard the interests of San Juan.

- Up to the time of going to press, the little son of Mr. and Mrs. R. J. Carson, of Durango, who so mysteriously disappeared last week, has not been found. The Italian beggar-woman has been liberated. The suspense of the parents must be terrible.

From the Dolores *News*: The Carson child has been recovered.

The Bartholdi Statue of Liberty Enlightening the World has been shipped from France. It weighs 220 tons; 188 tons are copper and the rest is wrought iron. The forefinger is eight feet long and four feet in circumference at the second joint. The head is fourteen and one-half feet high and the nose three feet seven inches long. The statue is 151.2 feet high.

- June 13, 1885 -

The high winds of the past ten days are liable to continue until the rainy season sets in.

Charlie Barstow's rig was implicated in another runaway last Sunday evening while picking up the pieces of the wreck on the week previous.

Arthur K. Patten, of Wagonwheel Gap, was in the city Tuesday. Mr. Patten is ready to entertain visitors at the Gap Hotel.

San Juan Siftings
- Alamosa is working up a bean bake.
- Montrose has been called the "City of Destiny."

- Silverton ladies are organizing a lawn tennis club.
- High water ran into the streets of Alamosa last week.
- "Another fine opening for a young man to go through a course of hard work and starvation," is the way a San Juan newspaper refers to a newspaper outfit for sale in another town.
- The *Graphic* again appears athwart the dimming gloom with the usual doleful invoice of woe. It reminds one of an undertaking establishment without a corpse. "This is a very hard world, and all are bad — but I."

Mr. John Sullivan, the eminent Boston slugger, testified in his divorce case the other day that though he might sometimes have been intoxicated, he was never drunk.

- June 20, 1885 -

The chimneys for the Court House have been placed in position and add largely to the appearance of the building.

The county officials this week moved into the new Court House. The new quarters are cozy indeed.

San Juan Siftings

- A ferry at Alamosa was reported doing good business last week.
- It now looks at though every town in San Juan would have its own Fourth of July celebration.
- Edwards, who shot Garcia at Silverton last week, is out on bail. Garcia will be out — on crutches — in a short time.

- The *La Plata Miner* says there are quite a number of men in Silverton looking for work and praying they won't find it.
- The County Commissioners of La Plata County offer $500 reward for the return of R. J. Carson's little son, alive, within sixty days.
- There has been a terrible mortality among bees in this valley. Some ranches have lost every colony. It has so far baffled the skill of those best posted. The latest cause for the mortality is thought to be the flower of the larkspur, which has been in great profusion since early spring. — *Durango Herald*

One of Rio Grande County's census enumerators recently met a probable grass widow who said she didn't know whether she was married or not. First, she left her husband and married again without a divorce; then the second husband left her and married without a divorce. She is in a quandary as to her exact standing in this respect.

- June 27, 1885 -

Summitville's census has just been completed showing a population of 354 people. (Henry paper please copy.) There is scarcely an idle man in the camp and consequently there are few loafers upon the streets. Snow in the town has almost disappeared. The Annie Company is doing the principal work of the camp. The camp supports four general stores, one drug and hardware store, half a dozen boarding houses, four saloons, two meat markets, etc. The road from Del Norte to Summitville is drying out rapidly but needs work in many places.

- The young men of Saguache have formed a string band.
- The Ouray *Muldoon*, with twenty columns of advertisements, advised people to go to Montrose to do their trading.
- The Silverton *Miner* estimates the output of San Juan County mines for the present season at not less than two million dollars.
- The Henry newspaper man recently became quite familiar with "Prof. Wagoner" upon the train and entertained him upon college business, etc. Inasmuch as Prof. Wagoner has nothing to do with college matters and has not been upon the train enroute East, this bit of enterprise is somewhat odd.

The following account is given of the origin of the term eavesdropper: At the revival of Masonry in 1717, a curious punishment was inflicted upon a man who listened at the door of a Masonic meeting in order to hear its secrets. He was summarily sentenced to be placed under the eaves of an outhouse while it was raining hard until the water ran in under the collar of his coat and out at his shoes. The penalty was inflicted on the spot and the name has continued ever since.

JULY 1885

- July 4, 1885 -

There will be a fine display of fireworks on South Spruce Street tonight.

Owing to the Fourth of July, an uprising among the Utes, and the first of the month occurring during the week, the PROSPECTOR'S news columns are not as full as usual.

As we expected, our illustrious but illiterate neighbor, the Henry *Graphic* cannot discern the faults of its rhetoric, even when they are pointed out. This paper mildly criticized the *Graphic's* assertion that, "It is with difficulty that the sheep can be learned anything," not because of it's possible truth, but because of its faulty expression. If this is not understood by our lugubrious contemporary, diagrams of the situation can be had upon application to this office during business hours.

San Juan Siftings
- A matrimonial boom is in progress at Saguache.
- Durango is duller than ever before in the town's history, says the *Idea*.
- The attendance at the Young Men's Club at Silverton is falling off. It is said that the boys prefer their old haunts of sin.
- In the various San Juan counties the census enumerators

have ascertained that the job was not so much of a picnic as they had imagined. Had Job been a census enumerator, his stock of patience would not have gone half way around.

• The miserable lot of trash being unloaded upon the people by the Henry *Graphic* is nauseating. There is some satisfaction in the fact that the people are learning to distinguish between a newspaper and a sheet conducted for personal spite and gain.

- July 11, 1885 -

A large beer vat from Bingel's Brewery will be used as a tank for the street sprinkler.

The Early Bird excursion trains to Wagonwheel Gap will run every Sunday until October 25, 1885, beginning July 12. There has been quite a local demand for these trains, so popular last season.

San Juan Siftings

• Rio Grande County shows a larger population than Saguache County, according to census returns.

• "Shotgun Collins," a prominent citizen of Montrose, has just been convicted of murder in the first degree.

• The Durango cemetery is out of repair, the headboards down, and no corpse knows who his neighbor may be. There will be a surprise party on Judgement Day.

• Joe Selig, one of the founders of Montrose, will shortly make a tour of San Juan for the purpose of deciding upon the most effective method of advertising the towns of the San Juan country.

Six hundred undertakers met in New York last week. It is a little early, but we have no doubt this will be the largest burying party of the season. The proceedings of the convention are shrouded in mystery; but we learn that there were no deadheads present and that the convention adjourned in a body.

- July 18, 1885 -

If, as now seems probable, the gap between Espanola and Santa Fe will be built over by a railroad to connect with the narrow-gauge. It is not difficult to prophesy some changes in commercial centers. Denver will have a direct line to the heart of New Mexico and cannot fail to profit greatly by the advantage. Santa Fe, which commercially is now eclipsed by Albuquerque and other new towns, will regain her former ascendancy. Alamosa will become the undisputed metropolis of the San Luis Valley and a railroad center of no small pretensions. The Valley itself will be relieved of its annual surplus products of hay and potatoes which cannot now be shipped into New Mexico, where they would meet with a ready sale.

An Aspen man fishing with dynamite the other day blew his arm off. The joy with which the news will be received will in some quarters be tempered by regrets that he did not blow his head off.

Fourth of July fires in the United States consumed property worth six million dollars. It costs to celebrate.

- Silverton butchers have declared war.
- The wild ravings of temperance fanatics are said to be bearing fruit at Saguache. Good!
- Kneeling benches have been placed in a Silverton church to accommodate newspaper men whose lavender pantaloons were becoming soiled.
- A drunken Fort Lewis deserter named McGlenn, broke his neck by jumping from a bridge into an imaginary stream near Durango last week.
- Cute — from the new editor: "The PROSPECTOR advertises a burro for sale. Going to make a change on the editorial staff?" — *Alamosa Independent*

Charlie Williams, a bad man with a gun who has been spreading terror around the vicinity of Henry for some time, loomed up athwart the Del Norte horizon this week, armed to the teeth, and opened the bad by knocking down and beating a Mexican woman name "Camilita." Williams was promptly arrested by Marshal Case, taken before Magistrate Goodrich and fined $30 and costs ($43.85 in all), in default of which he will assist in street work at the rate of $2 per day, with temporary headquarters at the calaboose. The way of the bad man is hard in Del Norte.

The question of insect eating is assuming importance, judging from the letters daily appearing in your columns. I contribute my theme — Grasshoppers. In New Zealand, during the years 1861-67, I frequently partook of and often consumed wholly as a piece de resistance whole dishes of them. Our mode of preparation was simple, and from a subsistence point of view very efficacious.

Material: One bushel of grasshoppers and one-half gallon brine (pork preferred). Preliminary: Mix and steep two hours. Preparation: Boil together in camp kettle for twenty minutes, rinse in lukewarm water and dish up. Before eating, divest of the head and tails, etc., al shrimp, and take with regulation biscuit. Result: Delicious. —*London Standard*

- July 25, 1885 -

It is safe to figure on a rain every day nowadays, at from about 11 a.m. to 3 p.m.

Those of our citizens who did not visit the hot springs last Sabbath might have been found scattered along the Rio Grande, fighting deer flies and mosquitoes and catching trout. A ten to fifty pound catch is not an uncommon thing nowadays.

A law passed by our last Legislature requires the following notice to be posted in every saloon or place where liquors are sold:
"No minor or habitual drunkard allowed here."
These cards, neatly printed, are for sale at the PROSPECTOR office.

Justice Goodrich is a terror to evildoers. Offenders against the law can hope for a full benefit in his court.

San Juan Siftings
- Alamosa authorities are cleaning up the town streets.
- The Montrose brass band is now fully organized and the natives have taken to the hills.

50

- A new bridge will be built over the Rio Grande at Alamosa at the junction of Denver Avenue and Fourth Street.
- Wm. Mulholland, an old time San Juaner, recently lost a hand near Rico while fishing with giant powder. It was a good hand but he played it wrong and lost.

When U. S. Grant breathed his last on Thursday morning, there passed from the world the greatest soldier it has known since Napoleon. The South, which he conquered, and to which in the late years of his life he showed the warmest friendship, will mourn him not less than the North.

The silly newspaper season does not as yet seem to have struck Colorado, at least not the very silly season. So far as is known, no Colorado paper has this year republished the wonderful story of the mineral cave tapestried with gold and silver. This was a famous old-time chestnut, and its decadence seems to mark the dawn of a new era wherein geological possibilities will have little chance.

Joseph Taylor, who was hanged in Philadelphia last Friday, had made a record for himself that would have put him in a position of esteem and honor in some parts of the West. Previous to the crime for which he was executed, he had at different times stabbed seventeen persons and shot twenty-eight. The inference is that his life had not been altogether tranquil.

One of the most useful yet neglected of all the arts is that of lying in bed. The damage that is done by persons getting up is past all reckoning. All the mischief and crime, the counterfeiting and forgery, the murder and theft are perpetrated by parties who persist in getting up.

Early to rise? People who rise early are sure to catch malaria; the ground is full of half-hatched poisonous germs; the sun is not up and has not warmed them into life, given them wings and set them adrift. Poor mistaken man, he arises early, inhales them all; they fructify and poison his entire system.

Fancy a man getting up on a cold rainy morning and climbing high hills on an empty stomach and leaving his French coffee and hot rolls, poached eggs and oyster stew to eat — what? Why, dew. How long would this fellow last?

The early bird catches the worm. Yes, but the sharp boy knocked the delusion in the head forever and eternally when he said: "Father, there's the point — what did the worm get up so early for? He trifled with destiny, he tempted fate, he should not have done it."

AUGUST 1885
- August 1, 1885 -

This is the 600th issue of the SAN JUAN PROSPECTOR. This paper has seen Del Norte a bustling mining center of 2500 inhabitants and it has seen it a half dead municipality containing scarce 500 souls. It was here in 1878 when Del Norte, its people and frame buildings, seemed moving en masse towards the rising sun of Alamosa, and when it was only by lively and unremitting rustling that the paper did not follow the procession as far as the graveyard. Since those days our lines have fallen in more pleasant places. The PROSPECTOR is part and parcel of Del Norte. There never has been a citizen of this place ashamed of his home paper. We are happy and proud to be able to return thanks to the people of Del Norte and Rio Grande County for the substantial help received for our labors, some of it in good words but the bulk in hard coin. With this latter, we have equipped one of the best printing offices in Colorado and from it has published a paper of which we are not at all ashamed. As opportunity offers, it will be continually improved regardless of the profit and loss account for, though we are not strictly speaking philanthropists, we have a besetting ambition to stand as near the front as possible and prefer that position to dividends. If there are any newcomers in this county who have not yet subscribed, they are urged to invite the PROSPECTOR into their homes. Its weekly visits will from the start be held cheap at three dollars a year.

Casual scanning of the Eastern press will reveal the fact that the newspapers of the cultured East are rather more given over to low and abusive language than those of the rowdy West.

Del Norte is said to have more fine-looking women than any town in the State. — *Denver Opinion*

Football has been the all absorbing topic after supper at Del Norte recently. A miscellaneous assortment of sprained ankles, wrist and sore shins are among the general results.

San Juan Siftings

- The "Saguachers" defeated the "Hay Seeds" of Villa Grove at baseball. Score was 25 to 6.
- Rollins, the Paradox murderer, has arrived at Montrose and confessed his crime. He will probably get a fair trial.
- There was an attempt at rape last week. The *Muldoon* suggests "a committee with power to act" as the remedy.
- Over at Ames, one night this week, a fellow lost his burro train, $500 cash, horse and saddle, rifle, six-shooter and ranch in the San Luis Valley. Poker was the game he played with such disastrous results. — *San Miguel Journal*

- August 8, 1885 -

About sixty-five persons visited Wagonwheel Gap last Sunday on the "Early Bird." The hotels have been crowded of late.

The devotion of the wife of Williams, the [very bad] man recently confined in the Del Norte calaboose, is worthy of a better man.

54

During his imprisonment, she has stood by the grating until a later hour every night offering him whatever consolation she might.

The systematic malicious exploding of dynamite under the trains of the Denver and Rio Grande railway has reached a pitch when the entire State is deeply interested in its suppression and the proper treatment of the perpetrators. All the detective machines of the State and the city of Denver should be put in operation to detect the dynamiters. As yet the people of Denver seem rather lethargic concerning the matter. It is a fact that there are people timid enough to avoid going to Denver when in danger of being blown up on the way.

San Juan Siftings

- Roller skating has gone out of style in the majority of San Juan towns and the rinks are being turned over to other purposes.
- Antonito has been surveyed and a town company formed. Antonito is expecting a boom that we all hope will turn out a good one.
- Of the 383 convicts in the Colorado penitentiary but five are Democrats. But, it has been 25 years since we have had a chance to forage.
- When State Senator Galloway, of Paradox, goes after a murderer or stock-thief, he is pretty sure to get his man. His experience with Rollins lately puts another feather in his cap.
- It may amuse our readers to know that the *Colorado Miner*, a newspaper published at Georgetown, the oldest silver mining camp in the State, is making rabid attacks on the whole of San Juan country.

A minister at a recent wedding came very near being broken up right in the midst of the ceremony by the bride, a pretty, fragile young little thing and one of his favorite parishioners. She had insisted on the most rigid of the Episcopal church forms and her Unitarian minister had humored her. Imagine, then, his surprise as he dictated the line: "Promising to love, honor and obey," to have her distinctly alter her oath to: "Promising to love, honor and be gay," looking him directly in the face the while. He had some difficulty to control his inclination to laugh and not being prepared for the contingency, let it slip.

- August 15, 1885 -

The killing of trout by the use of dynamite cartridges in the streams of Pennsylvania has become a business of large proportions. Although there is in that State a law against the use of explosives for such a purpose — just as there is in Colorado — the law is freely disregarded and none are punished under its provisions. The Pennsylvanians are now agitating the project of forming vigilance committees to deal properly with the offenders. Half a pound of giant powder will kill every fish, large and small, within a hundred feet. Under the present state of affairs, a few years more will see trout fishing a forgotten sport in Pennsylvania. How many years will it take to bring about the same result in Colorado? This sort of brutal and lawless work is known to be habitually practiced in every good trout stream in Colorado. It is the duty of every person having a suspicion that anybody is dynamiting to lay the facts of his knowledge before the authorities. In Del Norte, he may rest assured that the matter will receive prompt and full investigation. It has been determined that dynamiting shall be made odious on the

56

Rio Grande, and the first man caught in the act will be very sorry that he engaged in the business.

A copy of the SAN JUAN PROSPECTOR will be mailed for one year, free, to the first couple in Rio Grande County not engaged prior to August 15, 1885, who marry between September 1 and December 1, 1885.

The rage for outdoor sports in Del Norte now runs towards quoits and there are already many admirers of the game. Mr. Nisbet organized a quoit tournament on the beautiful lawn near his house, in which a number of citizens competed. The players were indebted to Mrs. Nesbit for a beautiful refreshment consisting of ice cream, lemonade and cake, while resting from the game.

San Juan Siftings

- The wagon bridge over the Rio Grande at Alamosa is in a dangerous condition, the approaches having been washed out by high water, and several serious accidents have occurred lately.
- The citizens of Alamosa have petitioned the city council to enforce the ordinance against the "soiled doves" of that town.

- August 22, 1885 -

The raspberry season is here and it is now in order to organize parties for the fray.

A large flock of very substantial hitching posts have been planted around the Court House grounds.

County Commissioner Tom Wilson visited the Gap Tuesday. He said he went partly for pleasure and partly because his wife had a toothache.

The telescope for the observatory will be in Del Norte at an early day.

San Juan Siftings

- Alamosa, it is said, will soon have a cheese factory.
- Three men, named Vance, Hall and Lane, were recently convicted of fishing with explosives near Osier and were fined $75 each and costs, in default of which they are with the Tierra Amarilla chain gang.

What is to become of us! With the morphine habit making a host of liars; the quinine habit a ghostly band of nerveless, would-be suicides; the tobacco habit giving us a tendency to cancer; the whiskey habit taking people by crooked ways to early graves; the money habit filling the country with avaricious speculators, thieves and bank robbers; the office-seeking habit turning honest people away from honest work; it does seem we are generally in a bad way.

- August 29, 1885 -

Fishing parties are all the rage in Del Norte just now. Last Tuesday a jolly band of conspirators against the peace and welfare of Troutdom, at the instigation of Mr. E. B. Greenleaf and his good wife, went to a delightful picnic ground five miles up the river. They, with Mrs. Rogers, Mr. and Mrs. Cooper, Mrs. Clayton, Mr. and Morse Chase, Mrs. Barclay and Mrs. Hill, boarded the "big bus" and fled from the bustling city with the expressed intention of having a good time. They were fully armed with

Cakes and wines

Hooks and Lines

Things neither man nor trout declines

And the appetite proved that the whole armament was needed. Mosquitoes, bugs, snakes and ants, the usual picnic visitors, were conspicuous only by their absence and the returning party, at peace with themselves and the world, and with fishing sacks not empty, pronounced a unanimous verdict of thanks to Mr. Greenleaf for a day of real pleasure.

San Juan Siftings

- Colonel David F. Day, of Ouray, is in town. He used to be simply an editor but is now a mining millionaire with an income of $2,500 a day.

59

SEPTEMBER 1885
- September 5, 1885 -

Dynamite, from the Greek word Dynamos, meaning power, is simply nitro-glycerine. The glycerine is a product of animal fat, usually of hog's lard. It is the most powerful engine of destruction ever discovered.

The list of delinquent taxes for the year 1884 is presented to our readers in this issue. While not of interest to the reader, it is full of importance to the publisher and we ask the indulgence of our patrons for any lack of reading matter during the publication listed.

- September 12, 1885 -

R. C. Nisbet has recently visited Silverton and contracted a lot of potatoes from the San Luis Valley. Mr. Nisbet handled nine-tenths of the potatoes exported from the valley last year. He is a rustler in this line.

- September 19, 1885 -

With the advent of cold weather, there is sign of new life among the rollerskating fraternity of San Juan.

The country around Alamosa is reported settling up rapidly and that town anticipates much as the headquarters for an agricultural community.

The Logan colony, under the direction of T. M. Moore, is pushing work near Alamosa. The town is being laid out, houses and fences built and wells put down.

On Monday last, a trout was caught in the Rio Grande which, upon being opened, was found to contain a full-grown mouse.

Clerk Bassett has instruction from the County Commissioners to rent the Courtroom to any first class entertainment that may come along. This will be good news for our people.

The time for ringing the bell at the public school in Del Norte is as follows:

- First bell commences to ring twenty-six minutes after eight o'clock and stops at twenty-nine minutes after eight o'clock.
- Second bell commences to ring five minutes before nine and stops one minute before nine, as near railroad time as possible.

Frank Mason rode from Montrose to the Paradox Valley last week bearing a death dispatch to Frank Steele, a distance of 121 miles. With one horse and but two hours rest, he made the round trip in sixty-eight hours.

A racket is being raised in Grand Junction because the School Board, failing to secure a Principal for their schools who suited them for $90 a month, offered him $100 and got him, while there were plenty of applicants who would jump at a chance to accept the $90.

Chance for brick makers: If the brick had been here, Olsen would have put up a new building as large as the one he now occupies and the post office and Catholic church would have been brick. We will need brick in this city early next spring. — *Montrose Register*

Newspapers of San Juan

- The Rico *Record* has entered its third year and is reported prospering.
- Montrose has three newspapers, all very creditable efforts.
- *The San Luis Valley Graphic* (of Henry) is now printed at Alamosa and is very much improved typographically.
- Telluride has two very creditable newspapers, but the fact that they are at swords' points will not materially aid the county.
- Silverton has perhaps experienced as many newspaper changes during the past three years as all other San Juan towns combined — an indication of a crowded field.
- Rev. E. C. Brooks, former editor of the Henry *Graphic*, is now editor of the Canon City *Mercury*, with a heading "Mirth moves the multitude," is in severe contrast with the tone of the paper.
- Capt. Henry Mingay has greatly improved the Saguache *Advance* and the name will be changed to the Saguache *Democrat*.
- A very sensible move is the consolidation of the Alamosa *Journal* and *Independent* as the *Independent-Journal*. The name is cumbersome but the principle of consolidation is right. There are too many high column newspapers starving to death in five columns towns.

- The Ouray *Muldoon* is still offered for sale. Colorado will never have another *Muldoon* and the wonder is that Mr. Day was so successful with a newspaper bearing this name. The man made the paper.
- Silverton indulged in a daily newspaper during a portion of the past summer. Upon its first appearance, early in the spring, the PROSPECTOR ventured the assertion that *The Daily* would curl up and die about the first fly of snow. *The Daily* retorted as follows in the issue of April 13th.
- The Del Norte PROSPECTOR, a paper published in a town that is nearly dead, predicts that a daily paper cannot thrive in a lively and prosperous town the size of Silverton. The PROSPECTOR does not know what it is talking about. *The Daily Democrat-Herald* has not reached our table for about two months past. Is it dead?

If one-half of the newspaper outfits of San Juan were blown up, the other half would have a chance to do something for the country and the publishers.

Only one more week of the tax list, gentle reader. Have patience.

- September 26, 1885 -

There was a rumor current last Saturday that a family named Clements had mysteriously disappeared from the Lower Saguache. Murder was hinted at.

The game of chess with living characters, at the M. E. church last Wednesday evening, was well patronized and very successful.

Instrumental and vocal music and a very nice lunch were features of the evening's entertainment.

Every property owner who can raise the timber should build a good substantial eight-foot two-inch plank walk in front of his property. Del Norte is growing into an age that demands sidewalks in the place of dust and mud.

San Juan Siftings

- Girls cannot chew gum in the Rico schools, under penalty of expulsion.
- The mayor of Ouray, (also a hotel keeper) recently collected a board bill from a pair of absconding customers with a six shooter.
- Johnny Moss, who used to play the banjo in the different dance halls of the San Juan country and is known to most all old-timers, committed suicide in Aspen lately.
- Recently a fool cowboy in Durango, by the name of Hilton, undertook to swing a sixshooter on his forefinger. The gun was loaded and ever since the doctors have been probing around Hilton's groin in search of a stray bullet. The man is seriously injured but may possibly recover.

Saguache

Saguache is one of the oldest towns in the southwestern part of the state, and in the good old days when the rivalry as a supply plant was between that town, Loma and Del Norte, scores of freighters, prospectors and ranchers made this town their headquarters, entering the interior of the San Juan Valley via the Cochetopa Pass.

At present Saguache is rather at a standstill, though the many very liberal inhabitants of the place still entertain hopes that fortune may yet favor them. A better hearted class of people never lived than those at Saguache, yet there seems to be a lack of enterprise in the town, whether owing to hard times or a lack of disposition to improve, we are not prepared to say. It is very evident that there is need of new blood in the town, new capital, and a disposition to raise the town from its lethargy. Saguache mercantile interests have been damaged somewhat by the competition at Villa Grove (the end of the railroad track) where many go to purchase supplies. The town has a very creditable brass band, but no fire companies, no State militia or other like organization.

Away out on the edge of town, but visible to the naked eye, is Saguache County Court House, a very creditable brick and stone building of two stories. This building is not unlike that at Del Norte, in general style. It contains one large vault and very neatly arranged offices and court room, all supplied with modern furniture and presided over by a very accommodating the thorough crew of officials. The one thing that strikes the visitor after jaunt out to the Saguache Court House from town, and after locating himself in a cool and shady place while the perspiration is being mopped from his temples, is how the Courts House came to be located upon the town site at all. The natural inference is that the people of the county seat must have stood in with the County Commissioners.

A prominent writer, in the days of '76, in describing Del Norte's appearance, said that, "The town is a mile long and thin as a shingle." This will not apply to Saguache. That town is built in the shape of an immense cross with the Court House at the base, the *Chronicle* and *Advance* offices at the top, and Bingel's beer depot and Michaud's hardware store at the extremity of the right and left arms respectively.

Saguache has been made the butt of many heartless jokes in days gone by, partially owing to its being the home of a certain "Hebrew Pathfinder" and because it was not flourishing as the green bay tree. In casually looking over the land, we are led to believe that Saguache may some day have an opportunity of getting even with some of those persons who have been so apt to criticize her standing.

This issue winds up the tax list. The sale will occur on the 5th of October.

OCTOBER 1885
- October 3, 1885 -

The Saguache Murder

One of the most atrocious murders ever committed in the Southern country has just been unearthed at Saguache. We reproduce the following particulars from the *Chronicle* of the 25th instant, concerning this case.

The good people of Saguache were startled and horrified on last Monday by the announcement that a double murder had been committed down in the lower portion of the valley. Sheriff Henderson and a posse went to the scene and found the report only too true — a double murder had been committed which, while not so terrible as the famous Bender butcheries in Kansas some years ago, yet was of a nature almost equally as tragic. Saguache County has heretofore been noted for its peaceful law-abiding citizens and this terrible affair has shocked all classes. Our reporter has been enabled to gather the following particulars.

A Brief History

Marshall Clements, the son of the elder Clements and the party accused of the crime, came to this country from Ireland some five or six years ago, and a short time after came to Colorado and settled on Trout Creek, near Buena Vista. In the summer of 1884 his brother, Thomas, joined him from New York. The brothers, after a short time, wrote to their father in Ireland to come on and settle in Colorado. On his arrival, the father and sons concluded to settle in Saguache County in the fall of 1884, at a point below the town some 18 miles. In the interim, during the winter, Thomas H. Clements married a Miss Susie J. Young. The father settled on the land and Mrs. Clements, who had wealthy relatives in the old country, partly furnished the money to stock their new ranch home with cattle. It appears that disagreements soon took place among the new settlers on account of the son, Marshall Clements, who having lived in the country some time, pretended to know more of the affairs of life here than his newly arrived brother from the old country. Another reason, so it is averred, for the deep ill-will that sprang up in the family, was the further fact that the murdered woman was receiving remittances occasionally from her people in Ireland, which her husband, Thomas, was investing in cattle on his own and his wife's account. It is stated that other members of the family were to receive benefits from this investment. On further inquiry it is learned that it was Thomas' intention to leave the neighborhood as soon as he could purchase a new ranch somewhere in the valley. The reason assigned by Thomas for this action was that it was getting very disagreeable for himself and wife while his brother Marshall remained so near in the neighborhood. He did purchase a ranch four miles below the place on which he was living. On learning the intention of Thomas and his wife, Marshall became greatly enraged, or at least even more jealous of his brother's good fortune.

The Disappearance

The morning of the 17th day of August was the last time that Thomas and Susie Clements were seen alive.

Ferreting Out the Crime

A few days after the above transaction, a gentleman named J. H.

Lewis, of Chaffee County, a former friend of the family, called to see them in their new home and was informed that Thomas and Susie had left the place on the 17th of August without giving any intimation as to where they were going or what their intentions were. Mr. Lewis learned that they had not taken any of their belongings. Susie had been preparing a dinner on the stove which was half cooked. These circumstances aroused the secret suspicions of Mr. Lewis and he called again a few days later. From the statements made him by Mr. Clements and his son Marshall, he was led to believe that some foul, damnable deed had been perpetrated and determined not to let the matter rest. After making subsequent visits to the family and locality, he became thoroughly convinced that Marshall Clements, and perhaps other members of the family, were the authors of a terrible tragedy, which future events too sadly proved. On the 18th, Mr. Lewis, in company with a neighbor, came to Saguache and gave information to the authorities and caused a warrant to be issued for the arrest of Marshall Clements and the other members of the family.

Marshall Clement's Arrest

On Saturday last, Sheriff Henderson and Deputy Woodard proceeded to the locality to make the arrests. On their arrival they were joined by a large number of residents of that section and a thorough search of the premises was instituted but without success. Sunday was spent in the so-far fruitless search with no result but on Monday a slight clue was obtained in the discovery of some blood-stained sheets. Marshall Clements was immediately arrested and sent to jail under guard of Deputy Woodard.

Clements' Confession

In the jail on Tuesday morning, Marshall Clements made a full confession of the horrible crime to Deputy Sheriff Woodard. It is substantially as follows: On Monday, the 17th, he went out to the point where his brother was at work on the ditch, taking with him his breech-loading shotgun and while climbing a fence the gun, by some accident, was discharged, the contents taking effect in the back part of his brother's head, killing him instantly. He immediately returned to the house and told Susie that he had accidentally killed him and induced her to go with him to where her husband lay dead. On arrival there she turned to Marshall and said, "You have murdered Tom!" No sooner had the words been uttered than Marshall killed her on the spot. He then proceeded to tell where the bodies could be found, which was a few rods south of their north line and about a quarter west of their east line.

The Family Arrested

Deputy Sheriff Woodard proceeded to the spot indicated and discovered the two bodies. Upon this, Sheriff Henderson immediately arrested the elder Clements, his oldest daughter, Nana Clements, Kate Clements, and Ann Clements, the wife of Marshall. The prisoners were brought to town and placed under surveillance.

Finding the Bodies

After Coronoer Hickey's advent on the scene, the body of Thomas Clements was exhumed from a hole in the ground not over two feet deep. The body lay in a doubled up position and was very much decomposed. Further search was then commenced for the body of Susie Clements, which was finally discovered about twenty-four feet south of where her husband's body was found. It may be stated here that the matter of finding the bodies was extremely difficult owing to the sandy nature of the soil and was only accomplished by the aid of an iron rod being sunk in the earth. The bodies were exhumed and placed in coffins sent down the previous night. They were brought to the graveyard just below town and a coroner's jury composed. The jury, after taking some testimony, adjourned at 2 o'clock. The bodies of the murdered couple were then consigned to their last resting place.

Additional Notes

The body of Thomas when found had nothing on but a common cotton shirt. The body of Mrs. Clements had on her ordinary every day wearing apparel and a pair of heavy shoes.

Another matter in connection with this terrible tragedy is that Marshall had secured some $100 worth of jewelry belonging to the murdered woman and to which he acknowledged having buried in a post hole in an old, vacated corral. Sheriff Henderson secured the property and has it in his charge.

Later

The Coroner's Jury finished its labors this week and the particulars are made public. The decision of Judge Harris was to the effect that the evidence was sufficient to warrant the remanding to jail of the prisoners Marshall Clements, John Clements, Nano Clements, and Kate Clements. The prisoners were held without bail.

THOS. CLEMENTS, THE MURDERED MAN.

SUSIE J. CLEMENTS, THE MURDERED
WOMAN.

Thomas and Susie Clements, the murdered couple.

Del Norte is undergoing a chess craze, especially around the post office block.

San Juan Siftings

- Henry has a very creditable public library.
- Old bachelors at Telluride have decided that the 30th day of February is the proper time to marry.
- Saguache County has been all stirred up of late over the Clements murder case.
- The recent consolidation of the Alamosa newspapers has been appropriately referred to as a "paper wedding."
- Over 100,000 pounds of ore left Ouray for the railroad yesterday. Another big roll of "boodle" to the County's credit.

Pets of Great Men

The attachment which some men have formed for animals of various kinds is an amusing subject. When philosophers have had neither wife nor children, they have taken to hogs, horses, serpents, birds and even spiders.

- Goethe rarely passed a day without bringing out from the chimney corner a live snake that he caressed like a bosom friend.
- Tiberius, a Roman Emperor, also made an intimate companion of a serpent, which he trained to take food out of his hand.
- Augustus was exceedingly fond of a parrot, but still more so of a quail, the loss of which made him as sad as if he lost a battle.
- Honorius, another Roman Emperor, was so grieved at the

loss of a favorite hen named Roma that he would willingly have given Rome itself to bring it back.

- The Emperor Dominican occupied his leisure in catching flies.
- Louis XI, when ill, only found pleasure in an exhibition of dancing pigs, oddly dressed up, which were trained for his special entertainment.
- Richter was very fond of tame animals, which he constantly had about him. Sometimes a mouse, then a great white cross spider, which he kept in a paper box with a glass top. There was a little door beneath by which he could feed his prisoner dead flies. In the autumn he collected winter food for his little tree frog and his tame spider. "How I wish," he wrote once to his friend, Otto, "that you could have met me in the street. Then you would have seen my little squirrel upon my shoulder, who bites no longer.
- Henry III, of France, was so foolishly fond of spaniels that he used to carry a litter of them in a basket suspended round his neck when giving his audiences. His passion for these animals cost him on the average no less than one hundred thousand crowns a year.
- Charles I, of England, was also very fond of spaniels and the breed of his dogs is still famous in this country.
- The painter, Razzi, formed friendships with all sorts of animals and filled his house with squirrels, monkeys, Angora cats, dwarfs, asses, he goats and Elba ponies. Besides these, he had an enormous raven who gravely strode about among the other animals as if he were the exhibitor of this Noah's ark. When anyone knocked at the

74

door, the raven called "Come in" in a loud voice.

- Pelisson, confined in the Bastile, made a friend of a spider, which he tamed. The jailor, one day, seeing Pelisson take pleasure in contemplating the insect, crushed it under his foot and left the prisoner in distress and melancholy at the loss of his friend. Later, in the same prison, he made companions of six and twenty rats who inhabited his cell. He gave each of them a name and they learned to come to him at his call.

- The Marquis de Montespan had the extraordinary taste to amuse himself with mice when occupying the gilded apartment of Versailles. True, the mice were white and had been brought to him all the way from Siberia, but the taste was a most odd one, nevertheless.

- Cardinal Muxarin, the French Minister, employed his leisure in playing with an ape and Cardinal Richelieu amused himself with his collection of cats.

- The Poet Altieri was proud of his horses and took great delight in them.

- William Cowper, English poet, was at no time so happy as when feeding his tame hares.

The game of living chess at the Methodist church on Wednesday evening of last week recalls a similar game played by Tamerlane, the conqueror of Asia, with some titled opponent. The pieces were represented by slaves and appropriate costumes. In order to add zest to the game, whenever Tamerlane captured one of his opponent's pieces he caused the captive to be beheaded in sight of the spectators.

75

- October 10, 1885 -

As yet, there are no takers for the PROSPECTOR matrimonial prize.

One hundred extra copies of the PROSPECTOR were sold last week. The account of the Saguache murder, with a complete review of other news, did it.

The "Early Bird" train made its last trip to Wagonwheel Gap for this season last Sunday.

A large number of boys from the age of five to fifteen years may be heard upon the streets of Del Norte almost any night at a late hour. Boys who are at home after dark cannot get into trouble.

A man down in Missouri has just turned insane from licking stamps at a post office window. Newspaper men are withdrawing from post office contests all over the Union.

San Juan Siftings
- Ouray is to be lighted — the lampposts being of a style and pattern that were abandoned in Missouri in 1852. Nothing antiquated about Ouray.
- A monster sea serpent or some other kind of "critter" comes nightly from the Dolores River, in the Paradox Valley, and grazes upon Senator Galloway's Lucerne patch. Its track measures six and one-fourth inches across. Perhaps it is a Gubernatorial nightmare.

- October 17, 1885 -

Immense forest fires have been raging in the mountains south and west of Del Norte of late. A party of our people visited the top of Mt. Lookout last Thursday evening, by moonlight, to witness the conflagration. The sight was grand in the extreme.

The Saguache *Advance* has evolved into the Saguache *Democrat*. The *Democrat* is a neat, well-edited, newsy select, all printed at home. The *Democrat* may be one of the unterrified but it cannot be said to be one of the unwashed for it is as bright and clean as a new pin.

San Juan Siftings

- The Henry *Graphic* is laboring under the effects of an overflow of gall.
- John Adams, of Montrose, has received a patent for a cravat fastener. He will negotiate territory to the Ouray vigilantes.
- Montrose editors are getting warmed up. One editor announces that he will resent all person's insults outside of his paper and stakes his home and manhood on the result. How nice it is for brethren to dwell together in unity.
- Ouray was never so exciting: Butchers all indicted; tinhorns on the fly; editors enjoying a weekly roundup; married men in the hills; mashers working double shifts; parlor picnics seven nights of the week; beer two for a quarter; moonlight strolls; pie three times a day; and fifty-five tons of ore per diem coming down from the hills. Blessed Ouray! Thus sings the *Muldoon*.

- October 24, 1885 -

Wires are down this week, hence no telegraph. They will be in working order by next week.

The snow and rain of the past week are reported as having extinguished the fires in the mountains west of town.

The average mean temperature at Del Norte last Sunday was mean enough to keep our people indoors the greater part of the day.

San Juan Siftings

- Cashier Tarbell, of Saguache, raised an eleven pound turnip and is the hero of the day.
- It is rumored that T. C. Henry is about to open an office at Alamosa. What's the matter with the town of Henry?
- The "Sit-down-ye-d—d-monopoly-mawed-cannibal" story in relation to Alfred Packer and Judge Gerry is again going the rounds of the San Juan press. The story was a good one originally, but has been spoiled by age.
- There have been no new developments in the Clements murder case. The four members of the family charged with the crime are still in the county jail awaiting the action of the Grand Jury which meets next month.
- Little has been heard of the "tracks" in Senator Galloway's Paradox Valley lucerne [alfalfa] patch of late. The publication of so transparent a story seemed an encroachment upon space that might have been occupied by Mustang liniment cuts to better advantage.
- The trial of Packard, the cannibal, is being urged in the

Supreme Court as he has already cost the county of Hinsdale $7,500. He was sentenced to hang in 1883 but an appeal was taken and a stay of proceedings granted, since which time he has been confined in the Gunnison jail.

- October 31, 1885 -

The Episcopal church building is being rapidly transformed into a dwelling house.

Some of the Del Norte musicians have organized a string band and are practicing together. It is to be hoped that their efforts will be substantially appreciated by our citizens.

Eve of All Hallows
The evening of the 31st of October, Halloween, it has long been customary to celebrate in various ways. When the reader of the PROSPECTOR glances through this article, his mind may travel back to youthful days and he will recall fond recollections of many strange occurrences.

Perhaps upon this eventful evening in years gone by he has been a party to unhinging gates, swapping signs, or participated in some other caper pronounced correct for the occasion.

The essential part of the Halloween ritual in former times consisted in the lighting by each household at nightfall. Then the family reunion took place and before the merry blaze the names of the valiant dead were recalled. It was believed that their spirits then visited the earth and that the fairies were then especially propitious.

These traditions and customs survived even the advance of

Christianity. Under its influence these old time and ancient observances received a new meaning. Until within the last fifty years Halloween was universally observed, especially in the British Isles and many of the old traditions have come down to us. In England the newly engaged couples kiss each other under the mistletoe. Mistletoe at one time also was a recognized remedy for epilepsy, convulsions, etc., but as none of our readers are liable to those calamities, further information upon the topic will be unnecessary.

Many forms and ceremonies still linger the popular traditions and tell of a time, forever gone, when people were not as wise as they now profess to be, but probably fully as happy. In this day of stern reality these traditions are listened to and called superstitions but it must be remembered that they originated in the days of a home and fireside where the family gathered and lived for each other.

San Juan Siftings

- There is a rumor that the Saguache murderers will ask for a change of venue to Rio Grande County.
- A recent item of expenses in Garfield County reads: "Bathing prisoners, $49," to which the *Ute Chief* says: "They must have used Florida water, bay rum, and Cashmere Bouquet soap."

NOVEMBER 1885
- November 7, 1885 -

Gum chewing is a feature recently favored in Del Norte's church congregations. There are places where gum would seem more fitting. Imagine the feeling of a pastor in addressing a congregation of gum chewers!

The ladies of the M. E. Church will give a dinner on Thanksgiving Day between the hours of 12 and 2 p.m.

Election day in Del Norte passed off quietly. There were no brawls and good feeling prevailed to as great an extent as possible.

Contractor Tucker has commenced work upon the Summit Road at the summit of the range, thus getting the high work done before cold weather sets in. He anticipates completing his contract by December 1.

- November 14, 1885 -

The usual winter's sickness is settling in Del Norte — much of it the result of impure water. This is why Del Norte should have a water works.

Quite a number of ladies have called on the PROSPECTOR office recently and are ever welcome. The man who does the affable act is a trifle clumsy about it but does his best. Call again.

San Juan Siftings

- The trial of the Clements murderers at Saguache has been in progress this week and last. The prevailing opinion from the start was to the effect that Marshal Clements alone would be convicted.

- Murder as a fine art received a black eye at Silverton last week when one citizen emptied his six-shooter at another without drawing blood.

- Two centenarians exercised their rights of citizenship in Saguache at the polls — one aged 100 and the other 101. They are both hale and hearty and as lively as crickets.

- The Supreme Court of Colorado has reversed the decision of Judge Gerry in the case of Alfred Packer, the man-eater. Packer was sentenced to be hanged but a stay of execution was made until the Supreme Court could pass upon the constitutionality of the law under which the prisoner was convicted. The case will be tried again on the charge of manslaughter.

A Necklace of Mummy Eyes

The material for a unique necklace is now in the hands of Messrs. Tiffany & Co., of New York and is awaiting the attention of their workmen. It consists of a large collection of very beautiful mummy eyes, which were brought from Peru by Mr. W. E. Curtis, of the South American Commission. The majority of them came from Arica, where large cemeteries are filled with mummies of the ancient Incas.

Some little discussion has occurred in scientific circles as to whether they are mummified human eyes or those of some variety of fish which had been substituted by the Inca embalmers on account of their less destructible nature.

On the other hand, Prof. Ramondi, the most distinguished native ethnologist, maintains that they are really human eyes.

Since they have been in this country they have been examined by several of the gentlemen associated with the Smithsonian and they seem to agree in pronouncing them to be the crystalline lens of the els of a cuttle fish or squid.

So common are the mummies that they can be dug up almost anywhere and can be purchased for four or five dollars apiece. In the rough state, the eyes are of a bronze yellow color but when the outer covering or skin is removed and the inner lens carefully polished, it becomes translucent and shows a handsome coloring varying from yellow to orange and reddish brown. In this form, it makes a very beautiful gem. The concentric arrangement of the different layers give the eye the appearance of iridescent glass.

The work of polishing the eyes has been interrupted by the illness of several of the lapidaries, which is attributed to poisons used in preserving the eyes. Some of the symptoms would indicate arsenic but the opinion has also been advanced that it is due to some alkaloid generated by the decomposition of the organic constituents. The illness of the workmen was sufficiently severe to produce an unwillingness to resume the task.

- November 21, 1885 -

Marshall Clements has been found guilty of murder in the first degree. That sounds healthy. — Aspen *Times*

Clements is sure to hang if Pete Breen can be kept out of the Governor's chair for a short time. Peter feels as though he ought to pardon somebody when he gets swing. If there ever was a just verdict, the jury in the Clements case rendered one. Of all the cruel, wanton, murders recorded in Southern Colorado, none is absolutely more uncalled for than that perpetrated by Marshall Clements. He will be hanged. Let the trap be sprung.

Marshall Clements will be hanged on the third day of December next. The affair will be the first legal hanging in the San Luis Valley within the knowledge of the PROSPECTOR.

San Luis Siftings

- The ladies of Telluride are adopting the short-hair system and the males are displeased.
- After living together for fourteen years, a Saguache couple have been indicted for adultery. The mills of the gods grind slowly, etc.
- The three members of the Clements family who were on trial and not convicted of the first indictment have been released on their own recognizance until such time as the District Attorney may determine what steps will be taken in the case.
- Quite a delegation from Del Norte will visit Saguache upon the occasion of the hanging of Marshall Clements.
- The new Summitville toll road company was organized Tuesday. As soon as the surveys are completed, work will be commenced and pushed along as the weather will permit. The route selected is a water-grade on the south side of the ranges so as to make it an easy grade and a road that will be open twelve months of the year.

The recent explosion in the Ball-Domingo mine, at Silver Cliff, whereby ten men lost their lives, is sad indeed. Giant powder had been stored in the engine room. Superintendent Ross has been severely censured for his conduct in storing powder in the engine room.

In a pack of cards with which two Chinamen had been playing poker at Stockton, California, recently, were found five aces, eight kings, six sixes, and other abnormal developments.

- November 28, 1885 -

Sheriff Henderson, of Saguache County, has very kindly tendered the PROSPECTOR a front pew at the Clements hanging. Marshall Clements still maintains his happy-go-lucky disposition and talks about going over the range with perfect composure.

A gang of hoodlum boys infest the streets of Del Norte at almost all hours of the night. No good can come of it.

The dinner by the ladies of the Methodist church, Thanksgiving Day, was well patronized and one of the finest public dinners ever served in Del Norte. When it comes to preparing a good dinner, the ladies of the M. E. Church know how to do it. They took in $80 which will be used in improving the church building.

The first discoverer of gold in the San Juan Mountains was a German girl named Bertha Wolf. She is now living in the southwestern part of this State and is said to be worth $100,000.

DECEMBER 1885
- December 5, 1885 -

The new star in Andromeda has been visible at Del Norte to the naked eye, of late.

Owing to a rush of business, the PROSPECTOR representative was unable to attend the Clements execution.

Marshall Clements was hanged this week. He deserved his fate richly, however, and there were no mourners among the multitude.

The hanging of Marshall Clements at Saguache on Thursday last was the first judicial proceeding of the kind in the history of the San Luis Valley. There have been several other occasions when capital punishment was inflicted but they faced the elements of court, judge, and jury. That Clements should have been hanged so soon after his crime is conclusive that the technicalities of law are not maintained to shield the guilty or defer their punishment. It is to be hoped that this salutary demonstration of the surety of courts in protecting the community from criminals will not be lost upon the people. There should never again be a lynching in the San Luis Valley. If juries will convict crime, law will punish it.

Del Norte's Observatory
The arrival of a portion of the monster telescope at Del Norte this week has created much comment. The whole instrument weighs

over a ton and will certainly be a great addition to the college. It will soon be in position and is certainly a monster in comparison with those of other observatories in the country. The manufacturer states he would not duplicate the Del Norte instrument short of $4,500.

San Juan Siftings

- Cattle will be allowed to roam at will in the limits of Alamosa the coming winter.
- The Costilla County people are at work building embankments along the Rio Grande to provide against high water in the spring. As a result, Alamosa is placed in a worse position than before as regards the overflow.

A farmer near Burlington, Wisconsin, was considerably exercised last week by the strange actions of a partridge which alighted on his head for three successive days while he was at work in the fields. His friends assured him that it was an omen of misfortune. On Saturday last he received word from the East that his rich uncle had died and left him a very large estate.

- December 12, 1885 -

There will be costumes sufficient for all for Christmas night's ball. People from the country and surrounding towns are especially urged to be present.

After the holidays, when advertising slacks up a trifle, the PROSPECTOR will be made better than ever. In the meantime, please read our advertisements.

- W. L. Williams, a Saguache photographer, is making views of Marshall Clements as he stood on the scaffold just before the execution.
- The snow slide season is here and the "death from snow slide" or "overcome by cold" items will greet the newspaper reader from this time until May.
- Very good photographs of the Clements execution are now on sale.
- A crazy man recently sent to the Pueblo asylum from Gunnison has written home that he is well pleased with the location "excepting for the lunatics."

- December 19, 1885 -

The entire telescope is now upon Lookout Mountain and will soon be in readiness for use.

San Juan Siftings

- Geo. White, of Parkville, Saguache County, died recently from the effects of a snake bite received nine years ago.

- December 26, 1885 -

Before being hanged, Marshall Clements gave a big goodbye to a Saguache lawyer and cheerfully added: "I'll meet you again by and by." The lawyer was so alarmed by the prospect suggested that he immediately purchased a Bible and prayer book. Unless he abandons the practice of law, the meeting will probably take place.

89

BYGONE STORIES
1886

JANUARY 1886

- January 2, 1886 -

Del Norte's holiday trade was good, better than for several years past.

The mail service from Del Norte to Lake City and from Del Norte to Villa Grove has been curtailed from daily to three times per week, to take effect during the present month.

San Juan Siftings

- Montrose has 280 children — mostly girls.
- Gambling is reported being practiced as openly as preaching at Montrose.
- Andy Hawn, of Ouray, was recently buried in a snow-slide in Diamond Gulch. No trace.
- Every once in a while you hear someone give utterance to the old saying, "A black Christmas makes a full churchyard," or words to that effect. — *Durango Herald*
- Silverton has indulged in another shooting scrape over some females. Nobody hurt. Colorado's next Legislature ought to make it a capital offense for a man to empty a six-shooter without hitting his man. This thing is growing monotonous.
- We notice that a large number of newspapers are still carrying the advertisement of G.W. Goerntio, of Erie, Pennsylvania, who offers to pay the highest cash price for

furs and skins. He is a fraud and does not even pay his advertising bills. — *Alamosa Independent Journal*

- Dr. Winters, of Durango, recently removed a tumor from the lip of a patient, successfully using the new anesthetic, cocaine, locally, as an aid to the operation. Cocaine is the article which Dr. Bradley, an Eastern physician, recently experimented with upon his family until all lost their reason or were ruined in health.

- January 9, 1886 -

During the past ten years, Del Norte has never known as good sleighing as is to be found here at present. It reminds one forcibly of early Leadville days. Del Norte is fairly jingling with sleigh bells about now. The town is always alive and up to the times.

The snow blockade on [La] Veta Pass last week is the first within the recollection of our people since the completion of the railroad.

San Juan Siftings

- The reward of $250 offered by the Southwestern Colorado Stock association for the arrest of John A. Smalley has been countermanded.
- The Alamosa *Independent Journal* says 2,000 people will be added to the population of the San Luis Valley in the spring.
- Money is reported very scarce but a matrimonial boom is reported sweeping over Saguache County that is appalling. The outlook for squalls next fall is flattering.

The largest land sale ever made in the state of Colorado, says the Denver *Tribune Republican*, has just been consummated in this city. It was of the "Luis Maria Baca Grant," situated in the northwestern part of the San Luis Valley in Saguache and Costillo counties. The grant contains 100,000 acres and was owned by ex-Governor Gilpin. The purchasers were Messrs. Adams and Mr. Gotthelf, of Saguache, though it is generally understood that the purchase was made for Eastern parties. The price paid is reported to have been $350,000, of which amount $200,000 was paid in cash.

Messrs. Adams & Gotthelf have occupied the grant for several years under lease and have devoted it to cattle raising. It is entirely enclosed by fences, contains some comfortable farm buildings, some cultivated fields and a large amount of hay land. The Grant, which is almost square, reaches on its eastern side into the Sangre de Cristo range where the grass grows luxuriantly, furnishing the richest of pastures. All over the grant the pasturage is good and its native grasses alone furnish food for fully 10,000 head of cattle. There are six streams of considerable importance running through it and half a dozen of less importance. It is said that they furnish water sufficient to irrigate 30,000 acres of land.

Its transfer is said to be an indication of the returning prosperity, which lends capitalists all over the Eastern country to seek profitable investment. It is believed to be only a forerunner of others which will soon take place in Colorado, bringing much needed capital to the state.

The curtailing of Summitville's mail service has produced a prolonged kick from people at both ends of the line. The fact is that Summitville is of entirely too much importance to be put off with a tri-weekly mail. During the summer season the camp has a population of from 500 to 600 people, all engaged in active business and to attempt to put this population off with a tri-weekly mail is an outrage. True, in winter there are not so many people in camp by half but nevertheless, the order curtailing the mail service to three times a week should be rescinded.

If some enterprising individual would make a snowplow that could be dragged by a span of horses, he could do a good act and make some money by clearing trails all over town.

Truly Del Norte is a favored spot. During the recent cold snap, the thermometer registered a greater degree of cold at other places in the valley than here. The town is in a basin, surrounded and protected by foothills. "Thirty-two below" is the wail from Alamosa.

- January 16, 1885 -

Old Sayings
As poor as a church mouse, as thin as a rail,
As fat as a porpoise, and rough as a gale;
As brave as a lion, as spry as a cat,
As bright as a sixpence, as weak as a rat.

As proud as a peacock, as sly as a fox,
As mad as a March hare, as strong as an ox;
As fair as a lily, as empty as air;
As rich as a Croesus, as cross as a bear.

As pure as an angel, as neat as a pin,
As smart as a steel trap, as ugly as sin;
As dead as a doornail, as white as a sheet,
As flat as a pancake, as red as a beet.

As round as an apple, as black as your hat,
As brown as a berry, as blind as a bat;
As mean as a miser, as full as a tick,
As plump as a partridge, as sharp as a stick.

As clean as a penny, as dark as a pail,
As hard as a millstone, as bitter as gall;
As fit as a fiddle, as clear as a bell,
As dry as a herring, as deep as a well.

As light as a feather, as firm as a rock,
As stiff as a poker, as calm as a clock;
As green as a goblin, as brisk as a bee,
And now let me stop lest you weary of me.

The PROSPECTOR makes a low bow to a patronizing public today. It is the PROSPECTOR'S thirteenth birthday.

The Denver papers have been asserting all the time that there has been no blockade on the mountain roads. This in the face of the fact that it has taken seventy-two hours to accomplish the distance between Denver and Del Norte. Possibly the train-hands held the train on the [La] Veta Pass just to enjoy the scenery.

As a result of the cold snap, one of Del Norte's young men has frozen on to a new girl.

The uncertainty of the mails during the past ten days [due to weather] had aided very materially in making life a burden to all.

Some of the newspapers are again harping upon Senator Bowen's poker playing proclivities. The public desires a rest upon this matter.

There is every reason for supposing that the bulk of the snow will lie on the ground until spring and in the meantime, another snow is liable to fall on top of it. The worst of the winter may come yet. Heavy snows are generally due in this section later in the season.

San Juan Siftings

- A package of Scotch snuff arrived in the Saguache mail last week and having been broken in transmission, set the post office force sneezing.
- Among gifts at a Montrose wedding last week were a dog, one dozen chickens, a riding whip, a saddle horse and a pair of "goose-ha'r pillows."
- The gastronomical feat of the Silverton miner who, on Christmas Day, ate three bowls of soup, half a turkey and a quart of cranberries, and cleaned up a score of side dishes and a bale of hay, is now going the grand rounds under the heading of "A Rocky Mountain Gorge."

97

Get out the coasters and toboggans. Del Norte will not have another such opportunity for years.

The PROSPECTOR'S suggestion regarding snow plows has been acted upon this week.

Our amateur actors should organize a dramatic troupe and entertain the town until spring. There is money in it and fun also.

All old soldiers and others will do well to attend the Grand Army drama to be presented in February. We are promised a rare treat.

During the recent cold weather and snow storms, it is gratifying to know that Del Norte's public schools and college are in a very prosperous condition. The teachers are untiring in their efforts and the success of the schools is assured at all times.

Articles of incorporation were filed in the Recorder's office of Rio Grande County last week for the town of Montevista, (sic) by J. P. Brook, J. W. Barrows, F.J. Skiff, C. H. Toll and E. P. Glass. It is understood that the name of Henry is to be changed to Montevista.

It is very evident that the Montevista people no longer care for the Henry attachment to the burg. The new name, however, is suggestive of a glimpse of the tiger and is hardly in keeping with the morals of the camp.

An additional fall of snow, accompanied by wind, gave Del Norte's sleighing a black eye. The roads around Del Norte are entirely too snowy for good sleighing.

San Juan Siftings

- Montrose newspapers are waging a fight against the carrying of pistols.
- The Saguache post office has been again removed — this time to the San Luis Valley Bank Building. Spoils of war.
- Bonanza, Saguache County, had a population of 5,000 people in 1881. Twenty-three families now form its total population.
- Dr. Harrison, of the Saguache *Chronicle,* says the Saguache *Democrat,* has been arrested. Something awful is hinted at.
- The noose that strangled Clements, the Saguache murderer, is now on exhibition at the Brunswick Hotel in Denver. It was sent to J. D. Cook, Chief of the Rocky Mountain Detective Association, by the Sheriff of Saguache County.

James Hotchkiss, on Sunday last, near Ouray, shot and killed a mountain lioness that measures seven feet from tip to tip. It is the largest one ever killed in this vicinity. It was bought by Tom Moore and Doc Rowan, who will stuff and put the animal on exhibition in their drug store.

- January 30, 1886 -

Snow shovelers have been in demand at [La] Veta Pass of late.

The PROSPECTOR narrowly escaped slipping up on the present

99

issue. We have a car load of paper somewhere down in the Kansas snow banks.

A very nasty affair has been unearthed at Saguache concerning some of the people of the town heretofore in good standing. The *Democrat* says, "Look out for breakers."

Mount Lookout has been alive with people of late — coasting, snow-shoeing, and having a good time.

The Commissioners of Rio Grande County very wisely appropriated $50 toward opening the Summitville Road this week. A force of seventy-five men has been at work tramping out a trail from the Summitville end this week.

San Juan Siftings

- Durango is reported to be the worst blockaded town in San Juan. The projections are that Durango will be blockaded for the rest of the winter.
- A snow slide on Mt. Sneffles, near Ouray, on Sunday, buried six men. All the bodies were recovered. Two were dead, one badly injured, and three slightly injured.
- By snow slides in the Mt. Sneffles district on the 17th, nine men lost their lives. This is the worst snow slide of the season.

FEBRUARY 1886
- February 6, 1886 -

At odd times lately several gentlemen have risen to declare that the backbone of winter has broken and have subsided upon finding their ears frozen.

The coasters have broken in a new hill and the toboggans now fly down Columbia Avenue. Harry Lee scored first blood. It requires about as much nerve and presence of mind to ride a toboggan as in managing a bucking horse.

The perils incident to mining in Colorado are fully as great as the dangers confronted by the coal miners in Pennsylvania. It is estimated that so far this winter between twenty and thirty men have lost their lives in this State by snow slides, and the full extent of the fatalities is not known. The snow is fully as deadly as the treacherous fire-damp. It is incomprehensible that cabins and mine buildings should be placed unprotected in the path of a possible slide.

San Juan Siftings

- Wagonloads of strawberries will be raised around Durango next summer, says a local paper.
- Quite an animated discussion is going on between Saguache editors. Is it about brethren dwelling together in unity?

101

- Lake City has a Young Bachelors' Mutual Improvement Club. No class of people on earth needs an improvement club more than the y. b's.

- February 13, 1886 -

Welch Nossaman, of Pagosa, came in on snowshoes Monday, via Summitville.

Owing to the illness of the pastor, the late Rev. P. McNutt, there were no services at the Methodist Church on Sunday evening.

Rev. McNutt died at his late residence in Del Norte on Tuesday, February 9, 1886, of congestion of the liver, age 53. He was born in Switzerland County, Indiana, August 27, 1832. He graduated at Asbury University, in Indiana, in 1856, and was married to Louise S. Slavena that same year. He has spent his life preaching and teaching. He was in the army one year, where he lost his health, and for twenty years his life had been a struggle with ill health and great bodily weakness. He came to Del Norte last May in hopes of benefitting his health, since which time he acted as pastor of the M. E. Church in Del Norte and Henry. His last act in his capacity as a minister was the establishment of a church at Henry.

He was truly a good man and no more genuine sorrow has ever been expressed in Del Norte at the death of anyone. Peace to his ashes.

General sorrow was expressed at Del Norte, both on account of the death of Mr. McNutt and because of the removal of his wife and daughter from our midst. May He who watches over all things be with the family and give them strength in their affliction.

102

The mail up to Jasper, Loyton and Conejos camp goes by snowshoes from Cockerel — a distance of from fifteen to twenty-five miles.

San Juan Siftings

- The old town of Henry now sails under the name of Monte Vista — two words instead of Montevista as many supposed.
- The last storm completely "snowed under," so to speak, all the storms of 1869 and 1884. It beat all previous records. — *Rico Record*
- A paper is to be presented to the Alamosa town trustees soon, forbidding, under penalty of fine or imprisonment, or both, any boy smoking a cigarette, cigar or pipe.
- Arkansas John, of Silverton, had his preliminary hearing on the 3d inst. for the killing of L. F. Telles, and was bound over in the sum of $2,500. Telles' body was escorted to its grave by a party on snowshoes, it being lashed to a toboggan.
- Rico people have just had a swell affair in a cemetery benefit, given at the house of a prominent citizen. A local undertaker, standing on a pall, called off the dances, making the necessary motions with his hearse plume; the collection was taken up in a miniature coffin, the leader of the German [dance] was attired in a shroud of the latest pattern, and the favors were black and white funeral rosettes and sprays of weeping willow. The order of the dances was headed by a skull and bones woodcut, and the last quadrille was, "Hark From the Tomb a Doleful Sound."

• From the Rico *News*: One of the largest snow slides which has ever come down a Dolores County mountain has covered up the mouth of the tunnel on the Ocean Mine being worked by Ben Hale and Sim Reveler. The slide started a mile and a half above the tunnel, near the ridge of Expectation Mountain, and mowed a path 200 yards wide all the way to the bottom of the gulch. The slide came down the day of the storm, and as the boys did not go to work until the storm ceased, they escaped. They estimate that the slide was 100 feet deep and in passing over the tunnel it deposited 35 feet of hard packed snow, through which it would not have been an easy matter to dig.

The following counties constitute what is known as the "San Juan:" Ouray, San Juan, Dolores, San Miguel, Hinsdale, Rio Grande and La Plata. Well may they be proud to be classed as part of the great "silvery" San Juan.

Cy. Munich was hanged at Leadville on the 5th inst. He protested his innocence to the last and took the opportunity to again curse certain parties instrumental in procuring his conviction. A mob of people in sleighs, on horseback, and on foot, witnessed the execution, breaking down the ropes around the gallows, and even climbing up to the gallows frame. There seems to be nothing improper about attending a public execution at Leadville — the entire population seems to have been present. On the return trip there were several runaways, if the press report is to be believed, and the corpse was dumped out into the snow. As a social event in Leadville, the Munich hanging has seldom been equalled.

Del Norte did not send very many Valentines this year.

San Juan Siftings

- Telluride men are reported troubled with the *embarrass de jambes* — whatever that may be.
- Ouray is in ecstasies over a new hearse just brought to town and costing $1,800. The *Muldoon* says: "It is equipped with all modern requirements, including a card case and a speaking tube to the driver, and as a tourist's carriage it is unequaled.
- Jim Leghorn, the cowpuncher from South Fork who rides a wooly cayuse from the plains, has recently been snowshoeing through the timber around South Fork. He reports it a difficult feat to pass upon both sides of a tree at once. [Editor's Note: Cayuse is an archaic term referring to a feral or low-quality horse or pony.]
- The Saguache *Democrat* says: "The Old Crow Literary Club of Carnero, meets every Saturday evening. Some of the members are apt to get full of — enthusiasm and are liable to get spilt."

The winter of 1885-86 will long be remembered all over the United States as one of the most severe the country has ever experienced. The heavy snows have been unusually destructive of human and animal life in the North, while in the South temperatures at or below zero have killed semi-tropical plants and trees as effectually as fire would have done.

The hanging of young Perry by a mob at Red Cliff seems to have been a most cowardly affair and devoid of any redeeming points. If Perry was guilty, the law should have had a chance. The day of the strangler is waning.

- February 27, 1886 -

The month of March ought to settle the heavy part of the winter in this section, though there were fourteen inches of snow in April of last year.

San Juan Siftings
- Wild geese are coming into the Valley and the old timer predicts an early spring.
- Henry advertises for bids to do the work of building a new brick church, 34x55' with a wing 15.5x35.
- Cattle are nipping the daisies from the graves in the Portland cemetery. The anti-fence law holds there.

Dr. Harrison was recently pardoned from the Saguache jail after serving two months of a three months sentence. Governor Eaton did it owing to the Doctor's ill health.

MARCH 1886

- March 6, 1886 -

The sun shone at Del Norte early on the morning of the first instant and a light snow was falling at the same time. Just whether the lion or the lamb could claim the day is a mooted question.

San Juan Siftings

- Chicken and clothesline thieves are raiding Ouray.
- Alamosa is after a flouring mill. Del Norte and Monte Vista, ditto.

Somebody has unearthed an old prophecy for the year 1886 of a decidedly uncomfortable nature. It appears that in the church of Oberemmel, near the city of Treveri, in Germany, there is a stone tablet some centuries old on which is cut the prophetic verse which in prose may be rendered:

"When Mark shall bring us Easter and Anthony shall sing praises at Pentecost, and John shall swing the censer at the field of Corpus Domini, then shall the whole earth resound with weepings and wailings."

Now it so happens that this year Easter falls on St. Mark's Day, Pentecost on that of St. Anthony of Padue, and the Corpus Domini comes on St. John the Baptist's day, June 24. Here then, are the first conditions of the prophecy fulfilled, so that non-believers in prophecies and anxious-minded persons generally have only to sit down and think of everything disagreeable that can possibly happen to this poor old planet and the dwellers thereon between January and December 1886.

- March 13, 1886 -

The Lenten season is here. Forty days of penitence! Fish and eggs are liable to take a boom.

Rio Grande is a highly moral county. No Grand Jury was summoned at the recent session of the District Court.

Go to the spelling-bee at the Presbyterian church this Saturday evening. There will be some spellers from Spellersville present. Admission, ten cents.

Rev. A. Crooks and wife and child, of Iowa, arrived in Del Norte last week. Mr. Crooks is the new pastor at the M. E. church.

San Juan Siftings

- It is stated that spring plowing is in progress at Silverton — snow plowing.
- The town board of Saguache has paid the debt of the town and now proposes to plant trees all over town. A good move.

- March 20, 1885 -

Who will be our next Mayor? Likewise Trustees and other town officers. Politics cut no figure in the coming municipal election. It is time to do away with petty political prejudices and work for the general good of the town.

Many of our people are of the opinion that the town should take some steps toward getting a new water supply.

Several days of the present week have been warm and spring-like, the warm winds and bright sun cutting deeply into the snow and causing the sod to assume a greenish tinge. Yea, verily, spring cometh.

Progressive euchre, now so fashionable, leads to many quarrels and as much cheating as the old outdoor recreation known as croquet or Methodist billiards. — *Register Call*

Rev. Darley's sermon last Sunday evening was upon the growing tendency among men to take God's name in vain — swearing, in fact. The evil is certainly a growing one and worthy of attention from the pulpit.

Myriads of snowbirds have been making headquarters at Del Norte this winter — thousands of them congregating in one flock. Last Thursday morning, while some parties were passing the corner of Sixth Street and Columbia Avenue, a flock of these pretty little chirpers passed overhead. Upon crossing the course of a telephone wire, there was a ping, jingling sound, and one of the birds fell at their feet, stunned by the contact with the wire. Many instances of this kind are recorded in the case of these birds, which have been known to receive very severe cuts and often meet death. The snowbirds referred to are very pretty, of a reddish-brown color about the body, and have black and white heads.

Bluebirds, the harbingers of spring, were noticed perched upon a Del Norte housetop this week, with a finest-climate-in-the-world expression on their faces.

Quite a fair-sized crowd assembled at the Presbyterian Church last Saturday evening to take part in or witness the spelling bee. The contest was quite interesting and the audience showed much pleasure during the evening. The prizes were awarded to Miss Amy Franklin and Wm. M. Maguire as the best spellers. The entertainment proved beyond a doubt that Del Norte has a lot of spellers who can undoubtedly hold their own under almost any circumstances.

A recent letter from Dr. Thomas, of the Pueblo insane asylum, states that the case of Mrs. Clemons is undoubtedly hopeless.

A colony of Grand Army people from Minneapolis have arranged to locate in the La Garita country, fourteen miles from Del Norte. The advance guard were in Del Norte this week and the balance of the colony will be along as soon as matters can be arranged concerning the town site, etc. The new town will be called Veteran.

San Juan Siftings

- The Rico "kids" have organized a fife and drum corps.
- A Silverton man is laboring with a device to fasten paper collars to undershirts.
- The Ouray *Muldoon* says of Montrose: "It has three newspapers, two variety shows, twenty saloons, two hotels, one jail, and plans for a church."

Del Norte this week quoted eggs at 25 cents and butter at 30 cents.

- March 27, 1886 -

Everything is Lent, so please do not try to borrow.

Del Norte has a baseball nine that is looking for a challenge.

Go around to the spelling bee this Friday evening. It is no disgrace to be spelled down and a nice present will be given to the winner. Try it.

Rev. Darley's sermon last Sunday evening should stir up some of our inactive citizens. Every man should make it a point to be of some value to the town.

> Some people go to church to take a walk;
> Some go there to laugh and talk;
> Some go there to sleep and nod,
> And a few go there to worship God.
> — *Sam Jones*

Why not celebrate Arbor Day in Del Norte? There is no place on earth where trees could be planted to better advantage. Look at Denver — one of the greatest charms of that city is the abundance of trees. Del Norte can be made proportionately charming.

Henry Born and John Teffi returned from Golden last Sunday, where they have been for a year, inmates of the Reform school. It is understood that the lesson received by these boys has had the desired effect and that they will endeavor to lead upright lives hereafter. In this very laudable purpose they should receive the assistance of every citizen.

San Juan Siftings

- There will be a big snowshoe contest at Silverton today.
- Six shooters, old bachelors and deadly original poetry are among San Juan's leading evils.
- President Moffat is quoted as having recently assured a Glenwood Springs man that he and his wife would ride into Glenwood in a Pullman car inside of twelve months.

Veteran City [The Grand Army from MN settled here. I think the issue before this one tells about it.] will be located about fourteen miles from Del Norte and there is a splendid wagon road all the way between these points. Why should not Del Norte supply the new town with the necessaries and luxuries of life?

Dr. Watson says that, "A sour loaf of bread is an immorality, containing in its ferment not only dyspepsia but profanity. What right has a woman to bake a dozen oaths into her dough!" Half of the family quarrels, he insists, are owing to the dishonest housekeeping of careless wives. But the doctor is a bachelor and bachelors are not supposed to know much about these things.

APRIL 1886

- April 3, 1886 -

Prepare to plant trees. A very little work by each property owner will add very materially in beautifying our town.

The Veteran City people are reported at work upon the new townsite. The balance of the colonists are expected soon.

The work of tearing away the old Metropolitan Hotel (known as the Howard House in early days) was commenced Thursday to make room for Shaw's new barn. The old Howard House was among the first buildings erected in Del Norte and at one time was the leading hotel in the San Juan country. Six-horse stages used to roll up in front of this noted hostelry and deposit their burden of alkali-covered capitalists, miners, or tenderfeet as the case might be. The house has sheltered wealth, beauty and innocence, and there is not an old-timer in San Juan who will not readily recall some incident in connection with the building. Its mission is finished and the building gives way to a more modern edifice.

San Juan Siftings

- Wagon roads entering Alamosa are reported in a fearful condition.
- During Tom Bowen's struggle for Senatorial success the *Muldoon* was his only organ, and his Ouray constituency among his hardest and most earnest workers. Today the

gang who branded him as an "adventurer" and "poker fiend" are doing the heavy slobbering and there is no species of taffy or fawning within their gift too rich for the "sagebrush statesman." Oh constituency, thou are as tricky as a mule. — *Ouray Muldoon*

At the spelling match, at the Presbyterian church last week, Mrs. P. F. Barclay was awarded the first prize and Mrs. David Knight the second prize. The contests in Del Norte thus far have developed the fact that men, as a rule, are poor spellers. Here is a golden opportunity for the ladies to laugh.

Young men in Nashville used to have a strange idea of fun. About twenty years ago, during a cold spell, they organized a society with fun as its avowed object. The fun consisted in raising money and distributing it among the poor people of the city and county. In the course of one winter they raised and gave away $17,000. The young men who were engaged in this frolic are now great headed but they maintain that they never in their lives enjoyed themselves as much as they did during that memorable winter. A few such practical jokes would be a blessing to every town in the United States.

- April 10, 1886 -

The Fourth of July will be here before we know it. Del Norte ought to arrange for a celebration of the day. It is none too early to begin talking the matter up.

There was no excitement over the election Tuesday, the following ticket being elected without opposition: Mayor — John Leghorn;

114

The Denver *Evening Times* says: "The Grand Army and the schools of the State will both join in the celebration of Arbor Day this year. The school children will plant for themselves for future enjoyment and the old soldiers in memory of fallen comrades. The suggestion is a happy one and should be generally complied with."

House cleaning and similar pastimes are now making life a burden to the average citizen.

The timber upon the streets leading to the railroad will probably be cut away this season so that passengers on the train may have a better chance to view the town.

Mr. Wilbur Shaw, of Del Norte, is constructing the largest and finest horse barn in all the San Luis Valley. The barn will be used for livery purposes and will be an ornament to that city. — *Field and Farm*

San Juan Siftings

- Saguache will soon have a public park with gravel walks, trees, lawns, etc.
- Officer Heck and a gambler named Creek emptied their pistols at one another last week at Durango. Both were wounded, Heck fatally.
- Andrew Newmeyer, aged 65 years, the keeper of the Half-Way House between Rico and Telluride, was found dead in his house by the mail carrier. It is thought that he was

115

murdered. Three years ago the lessee of this house was mysteriously shot.

- Jack Cunningham, the well known engineer on the D&RG between Placer and Del Norte, blew the whistle to his engine at Alamosa the other day until a wooden cigar sign across the way went into hysterics, all because there was a man lying on the track before the engine. Failing to scare up the sleeper, the kind hearted engineer stopped his engine and removed the obstacle — a dummy. April the first.

Veteran City Items

- The first party of colonists for this new town arrived March 15th. The platting of the townsite is still in progress. The town lots to be given the first thirty families are all claimed and houses will be built on them this season.
- A general store is to be started. A livery stable is talked of.
- A freight line has been opened. Two carloads of household goods belonging to the colonists have just arrived which will enable several families to go to keeping house.
- Breaking and plowing have commenced this week.
- Another party of several families is expected from Minneapolis next week to join the colony.
- Several tents are pitched by families who cannot wait to build.

- April 17, 1886 -

There was a light blow of snow last Monday morning — enough to whiten the ground.

Del Norte should take some action toward the establishment of a market day. These affairs have been very successful in other towns.

San Juan Siftings

- Veteran Cityites are buying supplies at Saguache, says the *Democrat*.
- A pair of alleged stolen pants created quite a stir in Alamosa last week.
- The second-rate gentry of the green cloth, otherwise known as tinhorns, are receiving pressing invitations to leave several San Juan towns.
- April 11, at 7:30 a.m., a fire was discovered in the second story of the Hotel Sanderson, Ouray, and in ten minutes the fire had gained frightful headway. At one time it seemed certain that the entire business portion of the town was doomed, but owing to the herculean efforts of one of the best fire departments in the State, ably assisted by the citizens, the fire was contained to the Hotel Sanderson, Allison's saloon, Cobb's restaurant, and Kelly's harness shop.
- Trout fishermen should use great care these days. Some of those parties who catch trout out of season may be made a horrible example of one of these fine days. It is no harm to carry a rod along the bank, but it is a crime to have fish in one's possession.
- The snow still holds its own in Summitville, with very little prospect of going off. The weather is very disagreeable.

- April 24, 1886 -

The PROSPECTOR feels duty bound to offer an apology to its many readers for its utterances of late regarding a syndicate with

117

headquarters at Monte Vista that has seen fit to misrepresent, malign and persecute not only the PROSPECTOR but many of its honest patrons. Had the PROSPECTOR ever given cause for such an attack, had it not ever aimed to work for the good of the people and the county, perhaps this apology would have been unnecessary; but now, being forced into a very distasteful fight by a conscienceless ring of unquestionably disreputable people whose sole object in the county is rule or ruin and the replenishment of their own purses, the PROSPECTOR will lay aside its mantle of dignity and use such means as lie within its power as a defense. Were the fight with other than the irresponsible and shameless syndicate that has sought by slander and otherwise to cast a cloud of suspicion upon many of the best known and most responsible men in Rio Grande County, the PROSPECTOR'S methods in this case would be vastly different. The PROSPECTOR has never sought this class of notoriety but after repeated abuse and slanderous assertions from the canal ring, finds itself forced to retaliate, for which it asks the forbearance of its readers.

Through the carelessness of somebody, Del Norte's paper mail was carried to Durango last Saturday. Such carelessness works a great hardship upon our people.

The town of Del Norte was never so thoroughly cleaned up as it will be this present spring. The Trustees are determined to leave nothing undone toward the perfect sanitary condition of the town.

Rio Grande County's citizens will perhaps never fully realize their obligations to Noah for having preserved the race of mankind by entering the ark until they have met the canal ring at Monte Vista.

Some of the gentlemen who are unsuspectingly being hauled around by the nose by the canal ring will realize their error one of these days.

The weeping philosopher of the Monte Vista triumvirate is still posing as the leader of a people who he is vainly endeavoring to make believe are in a wilderness. There is not a crying demand for this class of leadership.

The canal ring at Monte Vista has started the funding scheme and can see no convenient excuse of dropping it. In its dilemma, it is not unlike the party who, having caught a bear by the tail, screamed for help, that he might be given a chance to let go.

Mr. Neill, a foundry man from Denver, was induced to locate at Monte Vista some time ago with a good foundry plant. The ring made him a loan and the deadly mortgage will get in its work very shortly. The game is quite smooth and generally works.

The PROSPECTOR wishes it distinctly understood that it favors the earliest possible settlement of Rio Grande County and the San Luis Valley, but it objects to other than strictly honorable methods of settlement. A man who has been induced to settle in the valley and is then systematically robbed will never make a citizen such as we want. Honesty and fair dealing must go hand in hand with the settlement of the Valley.

"Spring — All hail," and rain and mud and slush. The bluebird is sidling up to its mate, trout fishermen line the river banks, the canal ring is lying for suckers, the umpire's season has opened up, and beer is thawing in Monte Vista cellars.

It has been suggested by citizens of Del Norte that Sixth Street be made the driving street of the town and that after it has been placed in order, no fast driving be allowed upon any other street in town. The scheme meets with much favor among many of our people who feel that Del Norte should have a Broadway.

San Juan Siftings

- Creek, the gambler recently shot at Durango by Officer Heck, is still alive.
- Dr. Harrison, formerly of Saguache, is now at Salida and is reported doing well. The Doctor, it is said, has turned over a new leaf and in his purpose should be aided by all.
- Shaveno, the Ute Chief, was killed by a brother Ute at the Ouray Agency on the 10th inst. The murder was promptly killed by friends of Shaveno and thrown into the river.
- Saguache County officials are reported whiling the happy hours away in shooting prairie dogs from the Court House door.
- From Carnero — Our camp is distressingly quiet. We have had over twelve inches of snowfall in the last forty-eight hours.

MAY 1886

- May 1, 1886 -

Remember the first Del Norte market day on the 8th!

Hail spring! The bedbug has stood upon the threshold of his domicile and been greeted with a slingshot or pair of brass knuckles, and the funny man has decreed that this is the time of year to sandpaper and turpentine old bedsteads and then burn them at the stake.

It is a matter of justice to state that the dishonorable fling at the Board of Trade that was recently given publicity through an alleged "citizens meeting" at Monte Vista, is not supported by the majority of the people of the eastern end of the county. That a few fanatics should lead a few honorable men into such a scheme is a case that calls for pity.

A new walk has been laid along the Sixth Street side of the Burton property. At the next meeting of the Board of Trustees of the town of Del Norte, it is expected that some action will be taken looking toward the construction of more sidewalks.

Some difficulty is reported among the colonists at Veteran and it has been stated that an opposition colony will be started by a dissatisfied element.

- Saguache has put out a large lot of trees this spring.
- Twenty-five hundred trees were set out at Montrose.
- Baths have been reduced to twenty-five cents each at Montrose and no takers.
- Montrose and Glenwood Springs are said to be the liveliest towns in Southwestern Colorado.
- J. R. Vance, of Salida, has established a soda factory at Montrose and the fizz, pop, bang of the pop bottle will aid in the summer campaign.
- Parties from Red Mountain who arrived at noon today report a death-dealing slide on the Mears Road between Chattanooga and Silverton, resulting in the death of the mail carrier and fourteen of Mears' mules. The point at which the slide is said to have occurred is known to be exceedingly dangerous. — *Ouray Muldoon*

- May 8, 1886 -

There were no services at the Presbyterian Church last Sunday evening due to the severe illness of Rev. Darley.

To the Editor: May I be permitted to avail myself of your valuable paper to express to the citizens of Del Norte my sincere appreciation of their sympathy and attention during the recent illness of my husband, and also to testify to the unremitting attention and watchful care of Dr. Rapp, by whose skill and judicious treatment Mr. Darley has been a second time placed in a fair way of recovery from a severe attack of typhoid pneumonia and brain fever. — Mrs. Darley

It is very evident that our contemporary at Monte Vista is not going about like a roaring lion so much as has very recently been its custom. It evidently believes in the old saying that, "He who fights and runs away may live to fight another day." There is not so much talk about thieves and syndicates as there had been previous to the late unpleasantness and the general tone of the sheet [newspaper] is that of one that has been convinced of the error of its way. It is fine sport to hunt the tiger but not at all amusing to change places with the tiger.

An unexpected heir promises to make things lively at Monte Vista before long. It is confidently expected that somebody will take to the woods before many days.

Contractor Carryl made a trip into Summitville this week. He reports the snow in many places almost as deep as the height of the telephone poles. How does this look for high water?

The Rio Grande River at Del Norte is already "riled," and the water somewhat higher. The spring rise generally comes about June 10 to 15th.

San Juan Siftings

- The Saguache papers have improved wonderfully of late in the quantity of local news. The fact that the people want the news in the fewest possible words is dawning upon many of our exchanges.
- Of the $203 collected for Silverton's public library, $186 was donated by the employees of the Silver Bell, Yankee Girl, National Belle and other Ouray mines.

- The prolonged screeching of the steam whistle on Monday night created a great deal of stir in town, it being regarded as a sign of distress. Subsequent investigation tells us that it was blown for a guide to anyone who might be out in the storm. — *Silverton Miner*

- May 15, 1886 -

The canal organ is glaring savagely toward Del Norte with a glare that would raise a blister on a cold chisel but it will never hurt Del Norte. The stony glare business has been played here before.

Fred Smith has made arrangements to burn 100,000 bricks at Del Norte this season and will begin work at once.

Rio Grande's output of lunatics was increased by one this week by the conveyance of Doc Stewart to Pueblo. Stewart was adjudged insane late Monday and was taken to Pueblo last Wednesday by Sheriff Cleghorn. Next!

San Juan Siftings
- Fifteen million bricks will be burned at Glenwood Springs this year.
- Some very nasty developments regarding land entries are promised from the vicinity of Monte Vista.
- Mrs. Van Cott, the renowned evangelist, threatens to visit Silverton. We trust the good lady will change her mind as that village is infested with a gang that the devil would decline even on commission. Try Gunnison or Colorado Springs. — *Ouray Muldoon.*

A lot of innocent ranchmen at Monte Vista are being made the unsuspecting tools of the canal organ through a series of meetings labeled "citizens meetings." Very few men are willing to acknowledge that they have been made fools of but it is a fact.

Another Valley Town — A company representing a colony composed of citizens from Michigan and Minnesota have purchased a townsite on the La Garita, four miles south of the new town of Veteran, and have commenced the work of laying out of the town. One hundred and sixty acres of land are being surveyed into town lots and will soon be complete. From information received, it would seem there is to be no delay in this enterprise, but that it will be pushed rapidly forward and settlers hurried in.

And now the stage line from Villa Grove to Bonanza is in trouble, if reports are true. Sometime between Saturday and Sunday the driver, Hank Brahman, left the county taking with him four horses and a buckboard. We understand that he reported to Superintendent Braley, at Villa Grove, that a heavy load would be brought in Monday morning and that he needed the above named property. It is rumored that he will return in a few days, the disappearance being simply to bring the stage company to terms as they are largely indebted to him. — *Saguache Chronicle*.

- May 22, 1886 -

The trees have just leafed out at Del Norte this week.

The Grand Army organization of Del Norte has inaugurated a movement to erect an appropriate monument in the cemetery at

125

that place to the memory of fallen comrades. [Editor's Note: The Grand Army of the Republic was a fraternal organization composed of veterans of the Union Army, Union Navy, Marines and the U.S. Revenue Cutter Service who served in the American Civil War for the Northern/Federal forces.]

The Monte Vista citizens' meeting presents the appalling spectacle of a collection of men fighting a debt that was created in great measure by the aid of the chairman of the meeting. What sort of consistency is this?

A New Line — The Del Norte and Villa Grove Through Mail and Express Company are getting matters in shape at Del Norte to place on the road the finest line of wagons and stock ever driven over the road. Three very fine wagons and a plentiful supply of horses are at Del Norte ready to go on the route July 1st. Daily trips will be made between Villa Grove and Saguache and triweekly trips between Del Norte and Saguache. This line will be prepared to handle all the passengers and express that comes over the road and will be in the charge of men who are thoroughly acquainted with the business.

San Juan Siftings

- Alamosans are directing travel to Taos via Del Norte and Mosca Pass.
- At Alamosa, the Rio Grande is slowly but surely raising and if it continues for a few more days, will be over the banks.
- Alamosa is endeavoring to get up a Fourth of July celebration, without horse races, etc., advocating the reading

of the Declaration of Independence and orations by fiery young orators. This is much like the play of Hamlet minus the leading character.

- May 29, 1886 -

A letter from Mrs. Anna Clemons to a Del Norte party states that she has wholly recovered her reason. Her physician advises her to go to New York.

Del Norte should have an ordinance providing a penalty for throwing any kind of slops or trash into the town ditches. Washing spittoons or thrown waste water in the ditches is hardly the right thing.

Here's an item: The bachelors of Del Norte are about to organize a club. It is generally conceded that no class of people on earth need a club worse than these people. Bachelors of thirty-five or over will be barred, while none will be admitted who cannot prove that he left the State because he had to.

Rev. Darley is not mending very rapidly and is still confined to his room.

San Juan Siftings
- Durango is lunging right ahead and promises to make an important city at no distant day. They are making a great war upon the dance house element of the city.
- Colorado has no law preventing corporations of foreigners from monopolizing our State and public lands, and there is

an entire absence of usury laws. — *Ouray Muldoon.*

- Able bodied men who have no means of support should not be permitted to loiter around Durango. They jeopardize chicken coops, log chains, doorknobs, and many other articles of usefulness. — *Durango Idea.*

- The *Rico Record* says a search is now being made nearly every day for the body of Hesse Musgrave, who was lost in a snow-slide in Horse Gulch last winter. As yet, no trace has been found of him. The tunnel on which he was working was dug out last week but nothing save his tools was found.

JUNE 1886
- June 5, 1886 -

Capt. Frank Thomas lost a finger joint this week in a dispute with a lady friend who rebuked him with a hand axe. Dr. Grubb performed the operation which left the Captain short one joint.

One of the prettiest homes in this section is that of John H. Shaw, just east of Del Norte. A large and comfortable house, surrounded by beautiful and well-kept gardens is a pleasing sight. The place is now occupied by Mr. and Mrs. Holloway.

William Bingel, the Del Norte brewer, contemplates putting in an electric light plant.

The memorial services at Del Norte were cut short by the falling of a very cold rain accompanied by wind.

Trains will now run to Wagonwheel Gap every day, including Sunday, in effect June 1. It will be a source of pleasure to our businessmen to note that the "Early Bird" (Sunday) trains so popular in years gone by, will be continued this season.

Monte Vista: The brick makers are fast preparing to burn their kiln and as soon as the brick are ready, the new Methodist Church will go up. The stone foundation is now being laid.

The Rio Grande has been unusually high for about ten days. This rise has come unusually early, at least three weeks early. All traffic from the north side of the river to this place comes by way of the seven-mile bridge.

San Juan Siftings

- Telluride will be left without a church shortly.
- The gamblers and scarlet daughters of Silverton are on the anxious seat and will be until after the Grand Jury adjourns.
- The Uncompahgre River promises to ignore the regular channel and visit neighboring ranches next week.
- "Indian David," of Montrose, now stands under charge of undue enthusiasm and familiarity with a neighbor's cow. He lies in jail and the pen yawns for him.
- The stage route between Del Norte and Summitville is impassable and the travel and traffic from the latter place is now coming via Jasper and the Alamosa Canon to Monte Vista. — *Denver Republican.*
- The PROSPECTOR has been assured that the road will be opened next week. The melting snow has made the road bad recently but the mail goes in via this route three days a week.

- June 12, 1886 -

Charles Young is putting down a walk of flagstones bedded in sand. This is the first walk of this kind to be laid in Del Norte and its completion will be looked forward to with interest. The borders of the walk will be constructed of large cobblestones set in the round. Mr. Young estimates that a good walk of this kind, twelve feet wide, can be put down for thirty-five cents a running foot.

Rev. Darley was out for a short walk last Tuesday. He is still in very feeble health and his hair has turned quite gray. His friends hope for his entire recovery at an early day.

The Rio Grande River has been on a boom down in New Mexico as well as in the San Luis Valley. The flood in Southern New Mexico, caused by heavy rains the past week, has washed away every bridge on the Santa Fe railroad across the Rio Grande River except at San Juan and Bernalillo. The river at places is two miles wide. The Santa Fe track at San Marcial and between Rincon and El Paso is gone. The old church of St. Francis, at the Santa Domingo Pueblo, over one hundred years old, has been washing away but the pictures and books in the building were saved, some dating back to the fourteenth century. As yet, no lives are reported lost.

San Juan Siftings

- Alamosans have been boating upon the slough on State Street of late.
- A fire at Durango, June 23, destroyed the dry goods and clothing house of Kruschke & Co. He will rebuild. The hardware house of Adams, Posey & Bayly was damaged $15,000, partly insured. The fire is supposed to have originated from the explosion of a lamp in Kruschke's store. It is not positively known that any person was in the store at the time the fire broke out. Mr. Kruschke was married only four months ago and went to Europe for a wedding tour. Returning, he was a passenger on the ill-fated *Oregon* and he and his wife lost all their luggage, valued at $5000.

Photographing dead people is a commoner thing nowadays than

one would suppose when photographs from life may be had so cheaply; but folks go along from day to day putting off the taking of their pictures or they forget it until sickness reaches out and gets them and the next thing their friends know, they are dead. A few hours before consigning their remains to the grave the relatives recall the fact that there is no picture and they rush out for a photographer.

A picture taken under such conditions as those found in the corpse room cannot be the best in the world. The casket must be uprighted and we have to do as well as circumstances will permit in the matter of light. Sometimes the eyes are pushed open but usually the remains are photographed as they appear in death and from that picture a life picture must be worked out by our crayon artist. I have made many portraits of dead people in that way. The charge usually made for photographing a corpse is $20, which of course does not include the cost of the crayon portrait.

- June 19, 1886 -

The people of Monte Vista, Alamosa, Summitville and other camps are earnestly invited to spend the Fourth of July at Del Norte. A grand time is expected.

R. C. Nisbet's fifty acres of potatoes are looking fine indeed. If there is anything Mr. Nisbet excels in, it is in potato raising.

Many Del Norte cellars contain water — the first ever known.

San Juan Siftings
• "Rough on Rats" has just been introduced at Alamosa.

132

- Delinquent newspaper subscribers are being harvested at Ouray.
- S. E. Jones, of Alamosa, will remove to Denver and branch out as a magnetic healer.
- The collection of tolls upon the road above Ouray is pronounced highway robbery by the local press.
- Shaw's Magnetic Springs, six miles from Del Norte, are growing in prominence. A number of almost marvelous cures have been worked very recently by the use of the waters.
- A large party of our people visited the observatory last Wednesday evening and were allowed the use of the telescope in making observations of Mars, Jupiter, and the moon. Refreshments were served.

The observatory Building - Lookout Mountain

- June 26, 1886 -

Let Del Norte business houses and residences be decorated on the Fourth of July.

Trout fishing is now quite good in the vicinity of Del Norte. A five pound trout is the largest heard from in Rio Grande County yet this spring.

President Cleveland fishes for trout with worms. Ugh! Such a man will hardly be re-elected.

Along with a lowering river and the trout fishing season, has come the playful mosquito. These little pests fairly bore a man to death along the river at any point from the Gap to Alamosa.

New members are being added to the Bachelors' Club every week. It is the intention of all to make this club an institution that will be respected. The aim of the organization has generally been misunderstood and an especial object of the members will be to build up for it a good name.

The PROSPECTOR has been unable to trace the rumor that President Cleveland and bride will visit Wagonwheel Gap this season to any authentic source. The President will find few more cheerful places during the summer.

Mrs. A. H. Leonard and four children had a narrow escape from drowning in the Rio Grande River at Del Norte last Sunday afternoon. There is a narrow piece of roadway just between the two bridges on the road to the north side of the river, and while passing along this road, the horse driven by Mrs. Leonard became frightened at some fishermen and backed or jumped off the bank into the river. The occupants clung to the buggy. The entire outfit, people and all, floated some distance down the river and were rescued by Messrs. Carryl, Kiel, McDonald, and Hathaway, who happened to be passing. Several lessons may be learned from this narrow escape, not the least of which is the fact that a good stout railing of some kind should be built along this dangerous piece of road. If possible, fishermen should be kept away from this very dangerous place as almost any passing horse will become frightened at a moving object at this point. If some steps are not taken, the PROSPECTOR may yet be called upon to chronicle a very sad case of drowning.

Miss Tillie Thompson, a young lady who happened to be in the party that were thrown into the Rio Grande last Sunday, deserves especial praise for having held on to the baby she was carrying in spite of being in the river. The child would have drowned but for Miss Thompson's exhibition of courage.

San Juan Siftings

- The Ouray *Muldoon* has been boycotted, owing to its position concerning certain matters in that town, but the paper still lives.
- The Attorney of Archuleta County receives $700 per year salary. This is undoubtedly the best salary paid in San Juan for like service.

- The *Miner* says that four-horse stagecoaches will be put on between Silverton and Montrose July 1. The trip to Denver can then be made in twenty-four hours, or just twenty-four hours sooner than by way of Durango and two dollars cheaper.
- It now turns out that the wife of President Cleveland has a pair of distant relatives in Durango and to get even with Durango, Silverton announces two pair of fatherless twins and the enforcement of the dog tax. Great strife between western towns.
- Rico's young men have lately organized an anti-marriage society called the "Misfit Club." Its aim is to guard against the fatal wiles of the villain cupid. — *Durango Herald.*

JULY 1886
- July 3, 1886 -

Rev. Darley is now able to be out though not as stout as of old. His sickness has extended over a period of nine weeks.

The PROSPECTOR'S subscribers are falling short of duty these days, else the springtime snake story would be forthcoming. Is it possible no large snakes have been killed since the snow went off?

San Juan Siftings

- Over 500 more men are in the Red Mountain district prospecting than at this time last year. — *Ouray Muldoon.*
- All the roads leading into Silverton are in fine condition and the town has again assumed its normal appearance, which means that the streets are crowded with jack trains, pack animals of all kinds and six-mule teams. — *Silverton Miner.*
- Last Wednesday night a fire was discovered in the Wathan House at Villa Grove, which was supposed to have been caused by the explosion of a lamp which hung in the main hall. Before the fire could be subdued, four buildings were laid in ashes.

Sam Jones, that veteran blatherskite, is still at large. The people are growing tired of this gentleman and for the sake of Christianity and the relief of a long-suffering public, it would seem to be the proper caper to place Mr. Jones on a reservation. The Christianity-for-revenue dodge is growing transparent. [Editor's note: A blatherskite is a person who talks at great length without making much sense.]

The young men of the land will be benefited by the recent discovery of a poison (tyrotoxican) in ice-cream, and the young ladies will be sorry to learn that it is extremely dangerous to eat ice-cream under any circumstances.

A reward of $5,000 has been offered for the arrest of the rustlers who killed William Ball, south of Durango, a short time since.

The Santa Fe *New Mexican* speaks rather lightly of the completion of the Texas, Santa Fe & Northern Railway. One thing is certain, there has been so much dilly-dallying regarding this proposed line that people are tired of it. It is time to lay the rails or cease the very monotonous talk about the road. It is time to shoot or give up the gun.

- July 10, 1886 -

The display of fireworks at Del Norte last Saturday was creditable indeed to the town.

Some very nice looking and palatable bread is being made from flour ground by the Del Norte mills. The process is the old fashioned burr process and it will surprise many of our people to know what excellent bread is being made from the flour.

The Shaw Magnetic Springs drew their proportion of the crowd last Sunday. It goes without saying that no finer bath or better supper can be had in this section. The plunge bath is a luxury not soon forgotten.

A red hot meeting of the Town Trustees was held in City Hall Tuesday evening.

- J. Cary French was appointed Police Magistrate.
- The office of Street Commissioner was wiped out of existence and the duties assigned to the Marshal at $85 per month as salary for the work of both offices.
- The Marshal was instructed to see that all sidewalks be built as soon as possible.
- All signs across sidewalks were ordered removed.
- Quite an argument was had relative to taxing boarding houses and the matter was laid over.
- W. H. Cochran presented a long petition praying for the closing of all business houses, excepting drug stores and livery stables, on Sundays. Petition was laid on the table.
- A large number of bills were acted upon.
- The present Board is distinguishing itself for the quantity of business it transacts in a given length of time.

A boy near the corner of Grand Avenue and Spruce Street, on the 3rd of July, blew the balcony of his pantaloons into the street beyond by carrying too much fire with a handful of fizzlers in his hip pocket.

Miss Cleveland's new book, *The Long Run*, has no reference to the 300-yard horse that was backed so furiously in a 600-yard race on the 3rd. If you must bet on a horse race, be sure you are "on the inside" first.

Variety is said to be the spice of life. Just for a change, the PROSPECTOR, you will observe, gentle reader, will work the silent contempt racket upon the contemporary at Monte Vista for this week only. Simply a letting go to get a better hold.

Trout fishing is now at its best in Rio Grande County. Everything bites readily — trout, mosquitoes, chubs, black gnats and green flies. The fisherman is at a loss whether to wear a mosquito headdress or dope his skin with camphor, pennyroyal, oil of tar or sweet oil. It is now in the height of style to wander up and down the river, accompanied by rod, reel, line, creel, wading stocking and a pickle and sandwich lunch. It is fun for the bugs and a pleasing pastime for man.

San Juan Siftings

- It is estimated that 2,000 people visited Saguache on the 3rd of July.
- Ed Howard, the man who has a national reputation as a consumer of lemon pies, has returned to Animas Forks.
- George Graves, an Alamosa brakeman, narrowly escaped death while repairing an air brake last week. His head was badly bruised.
- This thing of a young and handsome girl wasting her precious self upon a dried up specimen of the opposite sex, who cannot realize upon his real estate, is suicide. Girls! Girls!
- *The Durango Idea* is of the opinion that a man who, by word or deed, would influence the separation of man and wife,

could not be trusted to sit alone with his mother's corpse if she had a single gold filling in her teeth.

- One of the big ore wagons of the Mears Transportation Company was loaded at the Burro Bridge on Thursday with nine and a half tons of ore, and was hauled over Mears' tollroad by six mules. When it arrived at a point near the depot where the turn was made, it was hauled slightly from the track. Although the ground was perfectly hard and dry, the wheels on one side sank into the earth up to the hub. All efforts to budge it were futile and the wagon had to be unloaded before it could be moved. The weight of the wagon is 4,000 pounds making altogether eleven and a half tons as a load for six mules. The new wagons, which are ordered, are to be made with four inch tires which will assist materially to keep the road in condition.

- July 17, 1886 -

Rev. Darley has been spending a few days at the Gap recently for the benefit of his health.

It will be a difficult matter to find an enterprise of greater value to Del Norte and the San Luis Valley than the introduction of a full roller process for making flour. Some action has been recently taken to that end at Del Norte, and it is the earnest wish of all that the plan may succeed. It is enterprises of this nature that build up towns and make cities. Del Norte, with its thrift and enterprise, is the town of all other in the Valley to take the initiatory steps in the matter. The grain of the entire valley may yet be ground at Del Norte.

One of the most important matters in the history of Del Norte was the organization this week of the Del Norte Flouring Mill Company, with a large capital and the ordering by telegraph of the finest flouring mill plant that money will buy. The machines will be in operation within sixty to ninety days and will pay cash for the season's crop.

This mill will be run by water power from the Rio Grande River. People of Alamosa, Monte Vista, and Saguache are invited to send their grain to Del Norte next fall. We will be prepared to handle it.

There is nothing sleepy about Del Norte. Let the people remember that what she undertakes to do, she does with a snap. Our flouring mill is ordered and the money is up to pay for it. Congratulate us, neighbors. Whoopee!

"Richest is he who wants the least," is an old saying. If this be true, how poverty stricken must be our contemporary who wants the earth.

Arrangements are now complete for a shooting match between a team of ten men from Company B, Alamosa, and a team of ten men from Company G of Del Norte.

Will someone rise up and tell the people something about the building of the Santa Fe & Northern from Espanola to Santa Fe and Albuquerque? — *Albuquerque Journal*.

We can tell you as far as Santa Fe is concerned that the road will be in full running order before the snow flies next autumn. As to Albuquerque, that is further along. — *Santa Fe New Mexican*.

San Juan Siftings

- Brownie Lea has been killed again — this time at Silverton.
- The assessed valuation of Saguache County this year is $1,800,000.
- Silverton is still celebrating the Fourth of July. The people of that burg never did know when they had enough.
- Clint Dutcher recently killed his wife at Rico and then blew his own light out with a pistol. Domestic unhappiness.
- A Durango telegram of July 12, says: "The city has never exhibited so many signs of substantial improvement as at present. Building is going on in every direction and the demand for mechanics of all kinds cannot be supplied. Bricks are being made at the rate of 25,000 daily and there is not enough to supply the demand. Bricklayers are getting $5 per day and eight or ten more could get work. Business is booming in every department. The new buildings in the burned district are nearing completion and large new stocks of goods are arriving to fill these elegant stores."

Observations

- Contentment is better than money and just about as scarce.
- The selfish man has the most presence of mind. He never forgets himself.
- Vanity rules the fools and often makes simpletons of those who know better.
- Money is a handy commodity and it takes enterprise and self denial to get much of it.
- He who is the most slow in making a promise is the most faithful in the performance of it.

- Wickedness may prosper for a while, but in the long run he that sets all knaves at work will pay them.

- As we grow in years and experience, we become more tolerant for it is rare to see a fault we have not ourselves committed.

- Too many young men believe that the world owes every man a living and that it requires no effort on a man's part to make the collection.

A husband who has incurred the anger of his wife seeks refuge under the bed. "Come out you brigand, you rascal, you assassin!" screamed his gentle companion. "No, madam," he replied calmly, "I won't come out. I am going to show you that I shall do as I please in my own house!"

- July 24, 1886 -

A man who never writes of trout without using the term "speckled beauties" is abroad in the land. Squelch him.

Del Norte has ever been recognized as the head and front of the great section known as the San Luis Valley. While the town may not have grown as rapidly as some have wished, it has not gone backward and today we can report progress in many ways. [Long article about the history of the valley.]

The body of Mrs. Erowitz, who so mysteriously disappeared from a ranch above Del Norte on the 10th of June, was found last Thursday two miles below Del Norte where it had been washed up by the Rio Grande River. An inquest was held by Coroner Rapp on

Friday afternoon but owing to the late hour, full particulars could not be secured for this issue. The body had washed from ten to fifteen miles from the point where the woman is supposed to have fallen into the river.

San Juan Siftings

- Rico is the only town of any importance in the San Juan that has neither telephonic nor telegraphic communication with the outside world.
- The case of Alferd Packer, the well-known criminal, now in the county jail at Gunnison, will come up for rehearing this term of court in that city. A motion is prepared asking that the defendant be dismissed from further custody. The old interest in this famous case may be revived.

- July 31, 1886 -

The Coroner's Jury in the Erowitz case returned a verdict of death by drowning with suicidal intent.

Six to ten couples were out on horseback Friday evening of last week. This very healthful recreation is becoming quite popular of late. Such exercise will bring back the roses to the faded cheeks of our ladies and will clear the cobwebs from the brains of our businessmen. It has many advantages over dancing and the usual amusements. Let there be more horseback riding.

With all possible kindness toward those gentlemen who usually have charge of such matters, the PROSPECTOR suggests that in cases of postmortem examinations and like cases, the school boys and younger element generally of the town not be allowed as spectators of any part of the proceedings. No possible good can result to a boy of tender years witnessing the process of sawing the top of a corpse's head off or of delving among its intestines.

The outlook for Summitville for 1886 is anything but flattering and unless something occurs to work a wonderful change, next winter will be the dullest known for years in that camp.

San Juan Siftings

- Ouray is said to be well supplied with beets.
- The public "burrial" (sic) ground at Rico has been fenced and now presents a very creditable appearance.
- Baths cost 25 cents each at Glenwood Springs and are free to poor people.
- Some thief recently stole a pair of bellows, an anvil and a No. 8 cookstove from a miner's cabin in Prospect Basin. The stove is said to have had a fire in it.
- The Durango Town Council has sat on the Sunday baseballists and will allow no more playing upon that day within the city limits.
- Silverton was not provided with a Methodist pastor for the ensuing year. Few ministers would care to remain in that town over winter owing to the tendency of the altitude to wreck virtue.
- Reports are constantly reaching us of the frequent use of Giant Powder in the Rio Grande between Del Norte and Wagonwheel Gap. The scoundrels should be caught and strung up. — *Alamosa Independent Journal.*
- There has been no water running through the Alamosa

town ditch for the past week. The water in the river is about one foot lower than the bottom of the ditch. A gang of men is now engaged in trying to get the water through.

Boom in Stiffs

A Monte Vista special to the Denver *Tribune-Republican* of July 27 says:

- Two or three days ago Harry Franklin, living north of the Rio Grande River, found a skeleton in a pond on his place. Dr. Charles Welford examined the bones and said that they were the bones of a white man or perhaps a Mexican. Some think they were the remains of one of the two Mexicans who were drowned by the upsetting of a boat about a mile above Mr. Franklin's place in the spring of 1884.
- Another special of the same date says:
- The body of W. D. Starbuck, living east of the North Farm and about nine miles from Monte Vista, was found in his irrigating ditch yesterday, entirely nude. It is a matter of great doubt as to whether he committed suicide or whether he was murdered and thrown into the ditch. Some marks of violence were found on the body and great excitement prevails in the neighborhood.

AUGUST 1886
- August 7, 1886 -

"The Little Greys" were sold this week by Herman Krueger to a Monte Vista party. They have been in livery service in Del Norte for about eight or ten years and have earned more money than any livery team in the country. Many of Del Norte's young men are thankful that the "little greys" cannot talk.

Postmaster Hathaway reports finding a snake in his room one day last week.

Assessment of the Bank of Del Norte was raised $3,500.

Letters from the firm that is to supply the machinery for the Del Norte flouring mill state that the plans are finished and the machinery will be ready in a short time. Del Norte's mill is an absolute certainty.

Major Henry Foote was found dead August 6, from supposed heart disease. He was an old-time resident of Del Norte, a heavy property owner, and a member of the Del Norte Board of Trustees. Del Norte feels keenly the sudden loss of Major Foote both as a man and a citizen.

- The Packer case came on for trial at Gunnison before Judge Harrison on Saturday. The day was consumed in attempting to secure a jury.

- For reflecting upon the ancestry of one "Old Symes" at Montrose the other day, Bierkley, another local celebrity, had his jugular cut and died shortly afterward. Both men are spoken of as saloon bums.

- The body of Edwin J. Warner, whose death by drowning was noted in our last issue, was recovered on the 14th, four days after he drowned. The corpse was brought to the surface only a few feet from where he was seen last by sinking Giant Powder and exploding it on the bottom. — *San Miguel Journal.*

- Saturday last the body of D. W. Starbuck was found in an irrigating ditch. The supposition is that he went in to bathe at a time when overheated, was seized with a cramp, and sank at once. Mr. Starbuck has resided for some years past with Mr. Hathaway in the northern part of Costilla County. They were partners in the cattle business. — *Alamosa Independent Journal.*

At a ranch near Buena Vista a curious phenomenon is to be observed during thunderstorms. The stove upon which the midday meal is cooked becomes so charged with electricity as to render it impossible while the stove is warm to remove the cooking vessels. On touching the vessels, a severe shock is experienced and they adhere to the stove, resisting ordinary attempts to remove them.

- August 14, 1886 -

The turbine wheel for the Del Norte flouring mill arrived last week. The wheel weighs 12,000 pounds. The balance of the machinery for the mill is expected here soon.

Freedom has another shriek a-coming. The canal organ has been lariated and turned end over end for the fortieth time.

The physicians who embalmed the body of Maj. Foote stated that the very early decay of the body following the embalming process was owing to the fact that mortification had already set in when the body was embalmed. The record of these physicians in this line heretofore has been good.

San Juan Siftings

- Sykes, who killed Bierkley at Montrose last week, was committed to jail without bail. He is represented as a fly-blown bum of the first magnitude.
- Persons have often asked how long it would take a man to bleed to death after his jugular had been severed. The late Montrose incident places the time at three minutes.
- After three years in jail, Packer has finally been sentenced to forty years at Canon. Packer forgave everybody and will locate at Canon without a grudge in his heart.
- Perhaps San Juaners will learn in time to keep away from other men's wives. Chas. Trenchard has just had the life bored out of him with a Winchester by an outraged husband.
- Public sentiment is strongly in favor of exonerating the

man who killed Tranchard. Such tragedies generally excite more or less regret, but in this particular the regret seems to be that the affair had not occurred three or four years ago. — *Ouray Muldoon.*

• At last the costly and time-consuming Mason murder trial is ended. Frank Mason, the accused murderer of Cal Irwin, stands acquitted of the crime and once more walks the streets a free man. Some of the Jurors are credited with saying that the reason that they were in favor of finding a verdict of acquittal was because Cal Irwin called Frank Mason a s_ of a b_, and Frank had a right to shoot him. If this is a fact, it is a sad comment on Gunnison County for if this idea was carried out, the county would be depopulated in about three days.

The curious case of G. S. Edwards, who was struck by lightning while crossing Iron Hill at Leadville on July 4, is attracting considerable interest among scientific men. After the flash, Mr. Edwards remained unconscious for fifteen minutes before receiving assistance. The lighting struck him on the left cheek and after knocking out a number of his teeth, passed diagonally across the breast to the right side. It then descended the body to the foot, emerging from the right foot. It passed through the foot, leaving a hole similar to that made by a bullet. The clothing was torn into fragments, particles being found a distance of two hundred feet. Both of the boots were entirely destroyed and one of them carried sixty feet away. The ground where the man was standing was torn up for a considerable distance. The course of the electric current along the body was marked by a black and red streak one and a half inches wide. The worst effect of the streak seems to have been on the lungs. A severe hemorrhage was produced by which a quart of blood was lost. In addition to these injuries, the surface of the body was almost covered with blisters, the result of ugly burns. This, we believe, is the first authentic record of a person being injured by lightning at an elevation of 10,500 feet. It is remarkable that such severe internal injuries were not followed by death.

- August 28, 1886 -

The PROSPECTOR favors a waterworks first, last and all the time. Without pure water, Del Norte cannot hope to be the residence town of this section much longer. Give us pure water.

The same power that runs the waterworks pumps can be utilized for an electric light plant. Shall we illuminate?

The newspaper is a sure and safe index to the town in which it is published. Do we not mentally measure up a village or city by reading its newspaper? It is the traveling representative and advance agent of its town. It goes all over the Union and reveals the brightness or the stupidity of its home in a great degree. While this is not an infallible rule, it is safe to say that people will have about as good a paper as they are willing to pay for. In some instances, they get a better one. — *Bill Nye*

A surveyor from Denver has been in Del Norte this week surveying the grounds for a waterworks with a view to platting the same so that estimates can be made on the work. Del Norte will need a lot of men if the water works scheme goes through. There are no idle men here at present.

Rev. C. C. Zebold, the newly appointed minister, addressed a large congregation at the M. E. Church Sunday evening. The same sermon was delivered at Monte Vista in the morning.

The Del Norte rifle team was defeated again at Alamosa last Sunday making the requisite two out of three. They speak well of the hospitality of the Alamosa riflemen and acknowledge their defeat like men.

Snakes! James Gardner killed two immense rattlesnakes on the Francisco Creek Road Friday morning. Each snake measured fully three feet in length.

Our contemporary of late has been quiet upon those matters nearest its heart. It seems to be playing the part of "Dr. Jekyll and Mr. Hyde."

The press excursionists will be along this way soon after the 7th of September. If Del Norte is to entertain the press gang, something should be done toward that end at once.

San Juan Siftings

- Durango is to have a brewery.
- The press gang will soon invade the San Juan country.
- A third paper has been established at Glenwood Springs which makes two too many for the town.
- It is now rumored that Scott and Gibson, who recently ran a foot race in Silverton, are partners and are "working the producers" of San Juan.
- The Ouray dining room girls generally dress with more

taste and deport themselves in a better manner than those of their sex who are more presumptuous and less attractive. — *Ouray Muldoon.*

• Durango's electric light ordinance has passed and work will be commenced at once. Durango is an example of what enterprise will do for a town. The city is to have 24 lights for $4.16 per month each for ten years, to be erected at such places as the council shall designate. These lamps are to be lighted during the dark of the moon and cloudy nights, or as necessity may require, from twilight until dawn. The lights are to be cleaned, lighted and supplied with carbon by the light company.

The Saguache Chronicle, after an existence of twelve years, has died. The *Chronicle* was the oldest paper west of the Sangre de Cristo range in Colorado, excepting the Del Norte PROSPECTOR. The *Chronicle* material will be utilized at Leadville under the management of Dr. D. Helmberger.

SEPTEMBER 1886
- September 4, 1886 -

How about sewerage? The building of waterworks will require a waste way for water.

Scissors and paste. The press gang will be along next week. Del Norte has made no arrangements to receive them.

There was a heavy frost at Del Norte Wednesday night, with snow in the mountains. Old Baldy loomed up pure white on Thursday morning.

People from the surrounding country are already flocking to Del Norte for the fall and winter. Good schools will draw and Del Norte has them.

The Del Norte school bell has recently been cracked, some think by lightning.

For the first time in many weeks, Rev. Darley occupied the Presbyterian pulpit last Sunday evening, addressing a large congregation. The people trust that Mr. Darley's strength may be such that he can address them every Sunday.

Rev. Darley has pulled off his coat and will take a hand in building the addition to the college. The Presbyterian College of the

Southwest will be opened on September 10, for the fall and winter term.

T. C. Henry is figuring with the Del Norte sawmills for about 140,000 feet of lumber for use in building fifty houses on the big farm near Alamosa. The Del Norte mills are the only ones in the San Luis Valley that can fill the order in any reasonable time.

Our contemporary is going wild over the assessed valuation of the PROSPECTOR plant. Perhaps the change in administration of national affairs may have caused a shrinkage of the value of newspaper stock.

The miserable and uncalled for thrusts of the Monte Vista paper at the County Board of Equalization are without parallel and will meet their own reward. If Rio Grande County ever had a Board of Commissioners who tried to do right in these matters, the present one may be classed as such.

The Monte Vista paper could not use the Board of Commissioners to forward its selfish ends and hence turns loose the dogs of war upon that Board. The transgressor cannot always thrive. There will be a day of reckoning for our contemporary in its work of besmirching the character of honest men.

San Juan Siftings

- A red hot newspaper fight is in progress at Telluride.
- While moving the Saguache *Chronicle* outfit last week, one man lost the end of a finger while another had a foot smashed.

- September 11, 1886 -

The school bell has an exceedingly bilious sound these days. However, it seems to be all that it is cracked up to be.

There will be no excuse for ignorance about the children of today in the San Luis Valley. Send them to school.

The Monte Vista paper evidently is determined to slobber if it can't spit, and goes on each week with a lot of driveling rot over subjects of which it knows nothing.

San Juan Siftings
- Alamosa is making a kick on the price of coal — $7.50 a ton.
- The Montrose papers are enjoying a perpetual circus among themselves.
- Durango and Silverton have been arranging for the entertainment of the press gang.
- A hog of the feminine persuasion is said to be nursing a young burro at Ouray.
- Prospectors picket their burros in the streets of Silverton and use the doors and windows of empty houses to cook their slap-jacks and boil their coffee.

- September 18, 1886 -

The press excursionists stopped at the Windsor last Sunday evening. Charlie Coryell, Dr. Grubb and a number of our people were very active in entertaining the press gang.

Our contemporary at Monte Vista will be interested in the statement of Sam Jones that, "A man can afford anything better than going to Hades."

It is to be hoped the new bell for the school building will be along at an early day. The present bell, in its deranged state, is not calculated to inspire the young with the loftiest ambition.

The Del Norte Flouring Mill Company has been notified that the contract is made on freight for the shipping of the machinery, which will be forwarded at the earliest possible moment. All work in connection with the mill is progressing favorably and while the shipment of machinery has been delayed a short time, everything is all right. Later: The machines will positively be shipped from New York on the 22nd — next Wednesday.

The PROSPECTOR wishes it distinctly understood that it has no fight with the town of Monte Vista or its people, but will be found poking cold facts at the newspapers of that camp, so long as both papers are under the present management, unless there is a change of policy upon the part of the paw-paw organ.

The members of the Press Association left the San Luis Valley with the best of feeling toward Del Norte and the very rich section surrounding our town.

"Have you seen the moon?" was asked perhaps no less than a thousand times Tuesday evening along the avenue, as a big moon of a reddish color crept slowly up from the eastern horizon.

San Juan Siftings

- Durango threw in $400 for the press gang — money well expended.
- Ninety pupils were enrolled in the Saguache public schools last week.
- The tin-horn gentry have been notified to leave Telluride and Montrose is reported as receiving the crowd in a body.
- "Liver-nosed pirate" is the term applied to a Denver editor by a Durango pencil pusher. Neat but not gaudy.
- Glenwood Springs has made arrangement to put in a free bathhouse of ten tubs. There will be no excuse for the unclean in that camp.
- Owing to railroad washouts, Tucson has run out of potatoes and one of the hotels has on its menu: "Potatoes in a boxcar."
- Until a kid is old enough to discern between a kiss and a bite, courting widows is not safe. We are indebted to a feller from Siwatch (sic) for this chunk of information. — *Ouray Muldoon.*

Why Marry?

- Some marry for the fun of the thing and never see where it comes in. This is discouraging.
- Some marry for the sake of a good companion and never discover their mistake. This is lucky.
- Marriage resulting from love at first sight is generally wedded bliss on a par with sour milk. One or the other gets swindled, often both.
- Few people marry for pure love and they in after years suspicion that what were at the time promptings of tender

passion were, in all probability, but the first symptoms of cholera-morbus.

- September 25, 1886 -

The left-on-third-base tone of the *Graphic* is pitiful. It should take something — a walk perhaps.

Since it is the fashion, it would seem to be the correct thing for the *Graphic* to have its gall copyrighted.

San Juan Siftings

- Alamosa has a new town hall — pronounced very fine by those who have seen it.
- Silverton has watermelons in the market and frost on the ground every morning.
- Symes, the Montrose murderer, was lynched on Monday night last. "The Sheriff made a noble stand and several hundred shots were fired but nobody killed." Montrose is not noted for good marksmanship. Bosh! Why not tell the truth?

OCTOBER 1886
- October 2, 1886 -

The Bachelors' Club has arranged for a Pink Domino [dance] to be held at the Windsor Hotel Friday evening. Invitations have been issued. No person will be expected to take part in the dance, previous to unmasking, who does not wear a mask. A prize will be awarded to the lady and gentleman whom a committee shall decide to be the most graceful waltzers. The contest is open to unmarried people only. [Editor's Note: A domino is a mask, particularly a half mask worn at masquerades to conceal the upper part of the face.]

San Juan Siftings

- Alamosa is making a stand for artesian water.
- The attempt to establish a church at Telluride failed and the person who had charge of collecting the funds is returning the small amounts subscribed.
- It now seems that Symes who was taken from jail by a mob recently was not hanged but turned loose in the hills. Taxpayers are tired of paying for murder trials.
- The mail service between Glenwood Springs and Meeker is simply infamous. It takes longer for a letter to go to Meeker by the way of Ferguson postoffice, a distance of 65 miles, than out by Denver, Cape Horn, the North Pole and Rawlins, a considerably longer distance. Mail leaving here on Monday morning reaches Meeker the second Tuesday following. — *Glenwood Springs Chief.*

- The *Graphic* unloads a lot more rot regarding thieves, rings, robbers, etc., and the people snore on.

There are 850 recorded irrigating canals and ditches in the State, with a capacity to cover 2,000,000 acres of land.

- October 9, 1886 -

The new school bell is now in position. The tone is very similar to that of the old bell, though perhaps a trifle sharper.

Work on the new college building is progressing nicely. When Rev. Darley starts in on a building, it is pretty liable to go up.

Through the kindness of Superintendent Chritton, we were shown through the Del Norte flouring mills this week. Mr. Shull, the expert miller, is arranging matters in fine shape and when the new plant is in position, it is safe to say that the work will be thorough.

Everything is in readiness for the Pink Domino at the Windsor Hotel this evening. Before being admitted to the ballroom, all masked persons will be asked to remove their mask in the presence of an inspection committee, who will give each masker an inspector's check which, with their admission ticket, must be presented at the door. Dancing will begin at 9 o'clock. Oysters will be served by Mrs. Pim, just across the street from the Windsor.

Attorney Richardson had the extreme pleasure of totally annihilating the Monte Vista *Graphic* before the Commissioners last Monday. The first of January scheme did not stand fire.

162

- Uncompahgre Valley newspaper offices are being loaded down with watermelons of late.
- Joseph Selig, an old time resident of Montrose, will seek some sea level point as a method of saving his life, his health being very poor.

All who possibly can do should attend the Monte Vista Fair on the 15th and 16th. Our neighbors have worked long and hard to accomplish this much and are entitled to the good will and assistance of our people.

- October 16, 1886 -

The Pink Domino of last week was a very successful affair — there being, besides a good Del Norte attendance, many present from other parts of the county. The prize to the most graceful waltzers were given to Miss May Barstow and Mr. Ed. Eversole.

What will be the programme in Del Norte for the winter? Progressive euchre held fearful sway last winter. What shall it be this coming winter?

If Del Norte would take some steps toward the construction of a racetrack, considerable entertainment would be afforded our people at certain seasons of the year.

There is a prospect for an excellent race at Monte Vista on Saturday. A good track has been laid out and several horses are reported being fitted.

A woman living near Alamosa successfully manages, with the assistance of her daughters, a 320 acre ranch. Her crops have been large and good this year.

San Juan Siftings

- A miners' hospital is proposed at Ouray.
- Lake City is threatening to organize a dramatic club for the winter.
- Migratory birds have left for a warmer climate a month earlier than usual and certain persons have predicted an early winter.
- Symes, the Montrose murderer, who was recently taken from the Montrose jail and turned into the hills, has been recaptured and taken to Gunnison for safekeeping.
- James N. McLees, a gentleman who imagined it his especial duty to clean up a few of the peaceful citizens of Montrose, was found hanging to a crossbeam over the stockyard gate last Saturday morning.
- Montrose is tired of paying for the prosecution of murderers and criminals. *The Messenger* says: "Of the $112,000 indebtedness of Montrose County, $60,000 has been expended in the prosecution of murderers and criminals, leaving only $52,000 as the total expense necessary to run the county and build roads and bridges. Had we chopped off the murderous whelps long ago, what a fund we might have had to use in improving the county's highways."

Scraps

- Envelopes were first used in 1839.

- The first steel pen was made in 1830.
- The first newspaper advertisement appeared in 1652.

- October 23, 1886 -

Owing to the crowded condition of this issue, everything has been boiled down to the fewest possible words, except for the fair report. Our readers will bear with us for once.

Friday and Saturday were gala days at Monte Vista. The Fair and Exhibition of Stock, as advertised, brought hundreds of people to the scene and countless exhibits of all kinds were there for inspection. The general feeling among the people was that of surprise at the very excellent display made.

Del Norte's flouring mill is here and is being placed in position. Del Norte should indulge in a grand blowout of some kind upon the occasion of the manufacture of the first sack of flour from the new mill.

A branch of the Bachelor's Club has been organized at Monte Vista.

Senator Bowen left for Summitville last Wednesday clothed in the attire of a mining man.

Isaac White, the new town Marshal, is an old man in the business and will undoubtedly fill the position satisfactorily to all.

- October 30, 1886 -

It has been stated that the Texas, Santa Fe & Northern Railroad will be completed by January 1, 1887. The people of the San Luis Valley are certainly as anxious to have the road completed as the New Mexicans can possibly be.

The merchants of Del Norte are now laying in their fall and winter stocks of goods. The PROSPECTOR urges upon our people the importance of buying at home whatever can be had, even at a slight advance over Eastern prices.

Eighteen inches of snow fell at Summitville during the storm of last week.

The gay and festive collector of the root of all evil will be out upon the warpath next Monday.

We are appalled by the announcement that the ladies are figuring upon the organization of an Old Maids' Club.

The night of October 31st, of course all are aware, will be Halloween when it will be extremely fashionable to engineer all sorts of pranks upon the people. Looking in the mirror over the left shoulder, throwing the apple peeling, etc., will be among the performances. Our Scotch friends generally do Halloween to perfection.

San Juan Siftings
•   The citizens of Montrose have organized a literary society.

- Montrose has tapped a vein of soda water in the new artesian well.
- The voters of Ouray County will be called to vote on a proposition to build a $20,000 courthouse. The chances are that it will not be carried.
- Through the untiring efforts of Postmaster Houston, the mail connections between Glenwood Springs and Meeker have been greatly facilitated. Instead of taking two weeks to get mail from the Springs, it will now arrive in one week. — *Meeker Herald.*

The wager which we announced two weeks ago, as having been made at Animas Forks, that a burro belonging to Merrill Dowd could carry a load of 800 pounds a distance of 300 yards, came off last Sunday afternoon in the presence of the biggest crowd that could be rustled up in that section. About $2,000 was bet on the feat, which those betting on the burro won, as he walked away with the load as though it was an every day occurrence. — *Silverton Miner.*

The rink building has been removed from Lariat to Monte Vista and the Bachelors' Club of Monte Vista will give a dance in the building next Thursday night. Supper at the Mountain View Hotel. A fine time is expected.

NOVEMBER 1886
- November 6, 1886 -

It will be a relief to the reading public to know that the political writer will be shelved for a time. It is the news people want and in as few words as possible.

Rev. Darley announced from the pulpit last Sunday evening that he would probably not address his congregation after the 7th inst., for several months, as he is expected to go East in the interests of the college.

San Juan Siftings

- There are about twelve families and over sixty permanent residents on Disappointment Creek in this county, and still these people have no post office, having to go from twenty-five to forty miles (to Dolores) for their mail. — *Rico News Record.*

A lady died recently at the Georgia Asylum whose case was one of the most peculiar in the history of the institution. She was a perfect encyclopedia. She read voraciously and remembered everything she read. As she had means, she was indulged in the matter of books. She always bought from Lippincot. Whenever information was wanted in law, medicine or letters, she was appealed to and her answers were always correct. The legislative committee, on one occasion, was entertained by her for an hour. So impressed were the members with her accomplishments that they complained to Dr.

168

Powell for detaining her in the institution. "Just go back" said the doctor, "and ask her what she thinks of the Free Masons." They did so and found out that she was the craziest woman in the building.

- November 13, 1886 -

Some very entertaining cases are promised for the Grand Jury next week. Lightning may strike in high places.

A team belonging to H. M. Dyer paralyzed things in about two jumps at the back of Mrs. Van Liew's residence last Tuesday. No damage to the team or wagon but a small building was badly "discouraged."

A Western editor seriously remarks that he has good reason to believe that newspapermen become white mules after death because the expression on the countenance of a white mule has often reminded him of some deceased brother journalist, especially the despondent droop of the lower lip. He also calls attention to the fact that editors and white mules seldom die and are awful hard to kill.

San Juan Siftings

- Various San Juan towns are organizing literary societies for the winter.
- The salary of Silverton's town Marshal has been reduced to $100 per month.
- Lake City has a girl who blushes at the naked truth and won't examine facts until properly dressed. But the most modest of all was the young lady Uncle McFarland tells

about who wouldn't go to bed one night because the *Christian Observer* was lying on her bureau.

• Harte, the grocer, has sold upwards of 10,000 pounds of oleo the past season, and saved for the purchasers $3,500 which they would have paid for creamery butter. — *Telluride Journal.*

Capital Punishment by Electricity

There is now being exhibited at Leipzig an apparatus for putting criminals to death by electricity. So long as it is found necessary to retain capital punishment upon our statue books it may well be that the electric method is the most merciful and least repulsive process that could be devised for carrying the sentence into effect. But if such means are ever adopted in this country, the details will certainly not be carried out in the theatrical manner which commends itself to the Leipzig amateur. In this apparatus, behind the chair in which the condemned man is to take his seat, and by means of which his body is placed in circuit with a powerful coil, there stands a conventional figure of Justice with bandaged eyes, holding the balance in her left hand and the sword in her right. The criminal having taken his seat, the proper functionary is supposed to read over the record of his crimes and the sentence of the law. This ceremony completed, he folds up the document and places it in the scale pan, the arm of the balance descends, closes the circuit, and all is over.

- November 20, 1886 -

It is stated in railroad circles that 1887 will be noted for railroad building in Colorado. There are good reasons for supposing that a new line will enter the San Luis Valley from the North.

R. Lempke, who, by the way, is very much of a genius, has just finished a new switchboard for the Del Norte telephone line which is a very novel affair.

Dancing does not promise to be so popular at Del Norte this winter as usual. The parlor entertainment will rather take the place of dancing.

It is expected that the Del Norte Flouring Mills will be in running order by the latter part of next week.

W. E. Riddle, the clothing man, took a lot of orders at Del Norte this week. Del Norte men folks will fairly shine in about a month.

Postmaster Hathaway, of Del Norte, has received information of the establishment of a post office at La Garita with Joseph Gay as postmaster.

J. I. Howard, of Del Norte and a Monte Vista builder, have received the contract for doing the woodwork upon the Methodist Church at Monte Vista.

There is something decidedly fascinating in holding up to the people of other times the lamp of their own civilization and studying them in the light which comes to us, subdued by the flight of time and mellowed by the haze of distance.

San Juan Siftings

- A jaw bone four feet long has recently been found near Silverton.

- Silverton has organized a "Strawberry Shortcake Club," whatever that may be.
- A Montrose paper says: "Owing to the accident which destroyed one span of the State Bridge at Grand Junction some three weeks ago, the celebration and barbecue to be given under the auspices of the Board of Trade, which was advertised to take place on November 10, has been indefinitely postponed."

This incident may not be known generally to our readers and we venture to reprint it. When the unabridged edition of *Webster's Dictionary* first appeared (without a definition of the word unabridged), that great scholar, Caleb Cushing, wrote a criticism on the stupendous work saying that, for its size, it had as few errors as could be expected. This puzzled the editors who asked for an explanation of Mr. Cushing's information on the subject of those errors. In reply, Mr. Cushing marked 5,000 mistakes in the volume which had been presented to him and sent it back.

A New York scientist says that the earth's polar lee is penetrating the interior of the globe like a wedge and that as soon as it reaches the furnace there will be an explosion that will split the world into pieces too small for truck patches.

An Albia, Iowa, paper reports that a citizen grumbles because in a pound of butter purchased at a grocery he found three or four bedbugs, a number of red ants, and several long hairs.

-November 27, 1886 -

The more daring class of church goers fought their way to church last Sunday evening through a snow storm that came from all points of the compass. The evening was a terror to those Christians.

Landlord Brodie of the Windsor Hotel served up a fine dinner on Thanksgiving Day.

It is now quite the proper caper to appear upon the boulevard with a sealskin cap just over the intellect, or words to that effect.

San Juan Siftings
- Taffy pulling is all the rage in interior San Juan.
- Books are wanted for the Saguache School Library.
- A white deer was recently seen near Saguache.

DECEMBER 1886
- December 4, 1886 -

There is a powerful scarcity of wedding cakes at Del Norte this winter.

Last Sunday was a lovely day at Del Norte and many of our people took advantage of the day for a drive to Shaw's Hot Springs, six miles from Del Norte. These springs have wrought wonderful cures and have lost none of their popularity through age.

The large boiler for the Del Norte Flouring Mills arrived last week and has been placed in position. Why not have a whistle at the mills? There is no ordinance against making a big noise at the mill while the flour is rolling out.

There was a rainbow party at Del Norte this week, to which each lady brought an unhemmed apron. The gentlemen each were given one of the aprons to hem when he arrived at the party. One of our bachelors learned of the plan of the party (which was intended to be kept secret) and repaired to his room, tore up a good shirt to get suitable materials, and proceeded to rehearse the hemming act with a view to stealing a march upon the brethren and capturing the prize. He was fairly successful for a while then he suddenly slammed the work down and gave a bound out of his chair, at the same time quoting from the scriptures quite lavishly, all the while sucking the blood from the end of a finger that unfortunately happened to be on the opposite side of the muslin when the needle was pushed through. He spun around on one heel, howled, swore and worked himself into a frenzy. After tying up the bleeding member, the gentleman calmed himself and assaulted the work once more. He began humming "Sweet Violets" in an endeavor to appear calm. The steady stitching begat confidence as well as carelessness and the needle was thrust under the thumbnail. The artist gave a violent jerk and scratched his other hand with the pin that held the work fast to his knee. "Dash the infernal thing, anyhow!" he exclaimed as he tore the work from its mooring upon his knee and laid open a gash in a pair of $15 pantaloons where the pin was torn out. "I'll be blanked if I ever could sew and I'm a blankety-blanked idiot if I try to learn!" He kicked over a spittoon, threw the work in the stove and unbuttoned his shirt collar to cool off, falling into a chair almost exhausted. Calming down finally, the ridiculous part of the proceeding suddenly burst in upon his understanding and he broke out into a loud laugh, simultaneously with gazing into the mirror and exclaiming, "When will the fool killer be here, I wonder? A-hem." He then passed into the busy marts of commerce and began bartering for rum from a few companions upon the grounds of having just discovered that he was entitled to some consideration as a blooming idiot.

Update: The prize to the one who did the neatest work was awarded to Chas. C. Hathaway, while Mr. I. W. Schiffer was awarded another prize for a poorer piece of needlework, very much poorer. Two large tables were then spread and the repast was truly excellent. Dancing and a general good time followed, lasting until 1:30 a.m. The ladies of the S. N. M. club have reasons to feel very proud of their first party.

- Coal brings from $12 to $20 a ton at Ouray and a prolonged howl is going skyward.
- Alamosa depends almost entirely upon coal for fuel and the *Sentinel* is making war upon the rate that is charged for coal at that point.

- December 11, 1886 -

Old King Coal seems to be a very merry old soul in Colorado this winter. Leastwise he is drawing very much fire about now.

Senator Bowen is now in Washington. His Del Norte speech has shaken the State from center to circumference and there has been little unfavorable comment upon it. The Senator may not be re-elected but he will make the very best of the situation.

Ice skating is quite the fashion in Del Norte.

Holiday freight will soon be loading down the US Mails.

Rev. N. A. Chamberlain addressed a large congregation at the Methodist Church last Sunday evening. The gentleman spoke for an hour and ten minutes.

Send in your two dollars and get the PROSPECTOR for 1887. This is the oldest, largest, cheapest, and best paper in the valley and should be in every family.

San Juan Siftings

- Saguache sadly feels the need of a music teacher.
- Too many bosses are reported in the Telluride band.
- Mr. Hock and Miss Shock were recently married in Costilla County.
- Alamosa anticipates a direct railroad line north to Villa Grove.

What to Teach Our Daughters

- At a social gathering someone proposed this question: "What shall I teach my daughter?" The following replies were handed in:
- Teach her to arrange the parlor and the library.
- Teach her to make the neatest room in the house.
- Teach her that one hundred cents make a dollar.
- Teach her how to wear a calico dress and wear it like a queen.
- Teach her to say no and mean it, or yes and stick to it.
- Teach her to cultivate flowers and to keep the kitchen garden.
- Teach her to dress for health and comfort as well as for appearance.
- Teach her how to sew on buttons, darn stockings, and mend gloves.
- Teach her to having nothing to do with intemperate or dissolute young men.
- Teach her to regard the morals and habits and not money in selecting her associates.
- Teach her to observe the old rule: "A place for everything and everything in its place."

- Teach her that music, drawing, and painting are real accomplishments in the home and are not to be neglected if there be time and money for their use.
- Teach her the important truism that the more she lives within her income, the more she will save and the further she will get away from the poor house.
- Teacher her that a good, steady, church-going mechanic, farmer, clerk, or teacher without a cent is worth more than forty loafers.
- Teach her to embrace every opportunity for reading and to select such books as will give her the most useful and practical information in order to make the best progress in earlier as well as later home and school life.

Streetcar Manners

An observing woman in New York has been remarking on the number of women who said, "Thank you," to a gentleman relinquishing his seat in crowded streetcars. She took the period from January to June and in ninety instances only twenty-nine murmured an audible recognition of the favor. Eighteen mumbled something that might mean anything or nothing. The remaining forty-three accepted in silence and with aggravating indifference. Of the first class, twenty were brunettes; of the second, twelve were of light complexion, while in the last division only seventeen were brunettes. The observer argues that this proves there is more evident refinement and inherent politeness in the brunette than her fairer sister. She also observed that tall women are, as a rule, rarely thankful for the streetcar favors, while short women are profuse in their acknowledgements.

- December 18, 1886 -

The Del Norte Flouring Mills were started up and "primed" last Wednesday and considerable "chopping" was done besides. The start was made with water power. The flour turned out through the priming process is very fine but is not up to the standard of excellence that will be reached when the flour is run through the entire mill. President Crocker is highly pleased with the results thus far and is confident the mill will be a complete success. The slight delays caused by necessary work about the mill will soon be at an end and the "Del Norte Fancy" and other grades of flour will soon be in every home in the valley.

Rev. Geo. M. Darley was taken ill last week and has since been confined to his room.

The young men of Del Norte are willing to accept holiday gifts but they draw the line on scarfs and hat marks.

While making holiday presents; send a nice turkey around to some needy family. You will sleep better for having done good.

There should be a stringent law in Del Norte relative to keeping walks clear of snow. Keep the walks clean.

Some very excellent improvements have recently been made at Shaw's Springs in the private bath department.

A lunatic who was recently taken from Del Norte to the asylum at Pueblo, met a brother in the asylum. Neither had seen the other for eighteen years and knew nothing of the other's whereabouts. Then to meet in a lunatic asylum! With all their mental weakness, they fully recognized one another.

San Juan Siftings

- Silverton is reported duller than for years. Stores are now closed at 8 p.m.
- Frank Harwood, now eleven years old, was the first child born at Silverton. He was recently given a benefit by the people of that burg.
- Miss Delia Farley left yesterday for Del Norte, where she will spend the winter with her sister — that is, unless Madame Rumor proves true.
- The "winter widowers" in San Juan are flirting desperately these days. It's about time for Silverton to announce its holiday scandal.
- The Animas Forks Aldermen have ordered the construction of a new anti-freezing pump for the town's use. The natives are putting on metropolitan airs and refuse to drink out of the creek.
- It is said that the prospective metropolis in Montezuma Valley will be known as Cortez. It would have been called Montezuma but for the fact that there is a post office in Summit County by that name and the law forbids.
- Jack Williams, who a short time ago shot himself with suicidal intent on the La Plata River because his wife would not live with him, lingered some time and a few days ago, determined to die, shot himself in the head again and soon after died.

- December 25, 1886 -

The bulk of forty columns of good wholesome reading matter may be found in this issue of the PROSPECTOR. Send it East.

Rev. Darley is able to be out again.

The Del Norte Mills have been running this week and turning out some excellent flour. So far as heard from, the "Del Norte Fancy" is as good as the best.

The very decided change of tone recently adopted by Captain Aldrich toward the County Attorney would lead one to believe that the Captain anticipates making a meal of the Attorney at an early day. It is just possible also that the Captain has had some advice from the head office regarding etiquette and the advisability of indulging in a tumble.

San Juan Siftings
- Swine are reported loose in the streets of Alamosa.
- By order of the War Department the Cantonment on Uncompahgre has been changed to Fort Crawford in honor

of Captain Emmet Crawford who was murdered by the Mexicans while in pursuit of Geronimo.

- The San Diego fever, which was raging for a time here, has about died out, leaving those who remain here to rejoice in sunshine, peace and prosperity. Those who have emigrated will no doubt return again in the spring. — *San Miguel Journal.*

- Durango will be lighted by electricity by January 15th. The plant will start with a system of 600 lights, power for 1500 and present circulatory capacity of 850 lights. An eight room house will be lighted at a cost of $5.20 per month.

- A ghost on a white mule is reported making the grand rounds at the Uncompahgre cantonment every night. Somebody has stated that the ghost is that of a soldier who came back after his blankets.

THANK YOU!

Thank you for reading this book. I hope you found the journey back in time informative and entertaining. I know reviews are a pain but even a short review is helpful to me and to other readers, too.

Thank you to Galen, my husband of 51 years, and Donna Hass, my friend from college, for proofreading, suggestions and encouragement.

Thank you to the *Colorado Historic Newspapers Collection* (https://www.coloradohistoricnewspapers.org/) for their permission to use the online issues of the Colorado newspapers for this book. The collection includes 909,000 digitized pages from 200 Colorado newspapers published between 1859 and 1923. Are you interested in knowing some of the history of the state? You will find wonderful things in this collection. If you ever need information from a Colorado newspaper, this is the place to go. CHNC is a free site but they welcome donations of money and time.

Thank you to the Del Norte Museum for their assistance with photos and local history. The museum has an excellent variety of exhibits and a scavenger hunt for the kids.

Perk's coffee shop in downtown Del Norte is a good place to hang out while waiting for the museum to open at 10 a.m. After your visit, you can climb Lookout Mountain or go to the park and sit by the river or both. There is also a downtown historic walking tour and if you get hungry after all these activities, there are several good restaurants in town. I have found Del Norte a lovely and relaxing place to spend some time.

MORE BOOKS OF BYGONE STORIES

~Kindle Books~

BYGONE STORIES
FROM A TEXAS NEWSPAPER

BYGONE STORIES
FROM A VERMONT NEWSPAPER

BYGONE STORIES
FROM AN OREGON NEWSPAPER

BYGONE STORIES
FROM AN ILLINOIS NEWSPAPER

BYGONE STORIES
FROM THE ALAMOSA JOURNAL

CHICKENS IN THE NEWS 1872-1922

GHOSTS AND GRAVEYARDS
IN THE NEWS 1844-1922

MARRIAGE IN THE NEWS 1852-1922

~Paperback Books~

CHICKENS IN THE NEWS 1872-1922

GHOSTS AND GRAVEYARDS
IN THE NEWS 1844-1922

MARRIAGE IN THE NEWS 1852-1922

BYGONE STORIES
FROM THE ALAMOSA JOURNAL

~Coming in 2017~

BYGONE STORIES
FROM A KENTUCKY NEWSPAPER

Find links to all books on my Amazon Author's Page.

Visit 19thcentury-news.com for
More stories and excerpts from upcoming books

Made in the USA
Columbia, SC
11 June 2024

37004345R00119